Character Cake Toppers

Maisie Parrish

D&C
David and Charles

www.stitchcraftcreate.co.uk

I dedicate this lovely book to a very special lady, *Cathy Slatter*, for giving so much of her time and endless inspiration. My thanks also go to *Glenda* and all the staff at Cakes Around Town, Brisbane, Australia.

IMPORTANT NOTE

The models in this book were made using metric measurements. Imperial conversions have been provided, but the reader is advised that these are approximate and therefore significantly less precise than using the metric measurements given. By means of example, using metric a quantity of 1g can easily be measured, whereas the smallest quantity given in imperial on most modern electric scales is ⅛oz. The author and publisher cannot therefore be held responsible for any errors incurred by using the imperial measurements in this book and advise the reader to use the metric equivalents wherever possible.

Contents

Introduction

I am very proud and excited to present this new book, packed full of so much material to help and inspire you to create a wonderful range of cake toppers. As always, I have included lots of beautiful photographs and helpful step-by-step instructions – just the way you like it. With this in mind, I would like to tell you what makes this book different from any I have written before.

When I teach my workshops, I know from experience that my students are most interested in learning how to make the toppers and many travel from across the globe to do so. Most already know how to cover cakes and boards and want something more, so with this in mind, I hope I have delivered exactly what you are looking for.

There is something here for everyone to indulge in; some projects are very simple, while others are a little more testing, but I know that as you work your way through the book your skills and confidence will grow. Each of the 22 main projects include three separate items, making a total of 66 characters, animals, vehicles and accessories for you to mix and match for numerous occasions. At the back of the book, I have used three of the toppers to demonstrate how you can customize the designs on small or large cakes and bring in elements of the designs to use on boards and mini cakes.

I have discovered while making my toppers that Renshaw's white modelling paste is excellent for modelling work and I have used it extensively throughout. I am a great advocate of ready-coloured sugarpaste and there are some beautiful new colours in the Renshaw range to get excited about, perfect for mixing together with the modelling paste when you need to add colour. When a sugarpaste colour is unavailable, I have used Sugarflair paste food colour, which again comes in an amazing colour range. I also enjoyed using Rainbow Dust edible paints, which are water-soluble and look so pretty – their pink dust food colour is just perfect for dusting cheeks.

So now it's time to enter into the magical world of modelling with Maisie – lets make this journey together, and remember – everything starts with a ball!

Enjoy,

Maisie

Sugarpaste

Sugarpaste is a firm, sweet paste that is very soft and pliable and marks very easily. It is a very adaptable product and when it is used for modelling, especially for body parts or items that need support, we must add CMC (Tylose). All the models in this book are constructed using ready-made modelling paste wherever possible, as this is a most convenient and efficient way to achieve good results. This product does not need to have CMC added to it.

Note: Instructions for the Gingerbread Man can be found on www.stitchcraftcreate.co.uk

Ready-made sugarpaste

How lucky we are to be able to purchase sugarpaste in so many beautiful colours – just take it out of the packet and away you go! Of all the ready-made pastes on the market, the brand leader is Renshaw's Regalice (see Suppliers) and what a fantastic new range they have for us. The paste is very easy to work with and is of excellent firm quality.

TIP *Very dark colours, such as black, dark blue and brown, are particularly useful to buy ready-coloured, because if you add enough paste food colouring into white to obtain a strong shade, it will alter the consistency of the paste and make it more difficult to work with.*

Ready-made packaged sugarpaste is quick and convenient to use. Well-known brands are high quality and give consistently good results.

Making your own

While the ready-made sugarpaste is excellent, you can, of course, make your own at home. The bonus of this is that you can then tint your paste to any colour you like using edible paste food colour (see Colouring Sugarpaste). This can then be dusted with edible dust food colour to intensify or soften the shade.

SUGARPASTE RECIPE

- 900g (2lb) sifted icing (confectioners') sugar
- 120ml (8tbsp) liquid glucose
- 15g (½oz) gelatin
- 15ml (1tbsp) glycerine
- 45ml (3tbsp) cold water

1. Sprinkle the gelatin over the cold water and allow to 'sponge'. Place over a bowl of hot water and stir with a wooden spoon until all the gelatin crystals have dissolved. Do not allow the gelatin mixture to boil.

2. Add the glycerine and glucose to the gelatin and water and stir until melted.

3. Add the liquid mixture to the sifted icing (confectioners') sugar and mix thoroughly until combined.

4. Dust the work surface lightly with icing sugar, then turn out the paste and knead to a soft consistency until smooth and free of cracks.

5. Wrap the sugarpaste completely in cling film or store in an airtight freezer bag. If the paste is too soft and sticky to handle, work in a little more icing sugar.

QUICK SUGARPASTE RECIPE

- 500g (1lb 1½oz) sifted icing (confectioners') sugar
- 1 egg white
- 30ml (2tbsp) liquid glucose

1. Place the egg white and liquid glucose in a clean bowl. Add the icing (confectioners') sugar and mix together with a wooden spoon, then use your hands to bring the mixture into a ball.

2. Follow steps 4 and 5 of the Sugarpaste recipe for kneading and storage.

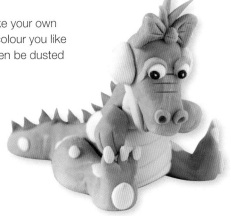

Sugarpaste is such a versatile modelling medium, it can be used to create an almost endless variety of cute characters.

Sugarpaste for modelling

To convert sugarpaste into modelling paste, all you need to do is add CMC (Tylose) powder (see Essential Purchases) to the basic recipe. The quantity needed will vary according to the temperature and humidity of the room, so you may need to experiment to get the right mix depending on the conditions you are working in. As a guide, add roughly 5ml (1tsp) of CMC to 225g (8oz) of sugarpaste and knead well. Place inside a freezer bag and allow the CMC to do its work for at least two hours. Knead the paste well before use to warm it up with your hands; this will make it more pliable and easier to use.

If you need to make any modelled parts slightly firmer, for example if they need to support other parts, knead a little extra CMC into the sugarpaste.

Throughout this book I have used the combination of sugarpaste and CMC powder, and find it works very well. If you add too much CMC to the paste it will begin to crack, which is not desirable. Should this happen, knead in a little white vegetable fat (shortening) to soften the paste and make it pliable again.

Colouring sugarpaste

Whether you choose to make your own, or to buy ready-made sugarpaste, the white variety of both forms can be coloured with paste food colours to provide a wonderful spectrum of shades.

SOLID COLOURS

1. Roll the sugarpaste to be coloured into a smooth ball and run your palm over the top. Take a cocktail stick (toothpick) and dip it into the paste food colour. Apply the colour over the surface of the sugarpaste. Do not add too much at first, as you can always add more if required.

2. Dip your finger into some cooled boiled water, shaking off any excess and run it over the top of the colour. This will allow the colour to disperse much more quickly into the sugarpaste.

3. Dust the work surface with a little icing (confectioners') sugar and knead the colour evenly into the sugarpaste.

4. The colour will deepen slightly as it stands. If you want to darken it even more, just add more paste food colour and knead again.

MARBLED EFFECT

1. Apply the paste food colour to the sugarpaste as directed above, but instead of working it until the colour is evenly dispersed, knead it for a shorter time to give a marbled effect.

2. You can also marble two or more colours into a sausage shape, twist them together and then roll into a ball. Again, do not blend them together too much. Cakes and boards look particularly nice when covered with marbled paste.

TIP *When colouring white sugarpaste, do not use liquid food colour as it will make the paste too sticky.*

Edible food colours come in a wide variety of forms – liquid, paste, dust and even pens – all of which can be used to add colour and life to your sugarpaste models.

Painting on sugarpaste

There are various different ways of painting on sugarpaste. The most common way is to use paste food colour diluted with some cooled boiled water, or you can use liquid food colours and gels. There are also some food colour pens available, but these tend to work better on harder surfaces. Another way is to dilute dust food colour with clear alcohol. I have enjoyed using a new product for painting on sugarpaste: Rainbow Dust food colour. It is a metallic range of water-soluble paint in the most beautiful shades. Just paint it on and give your work a really eye-catching look.

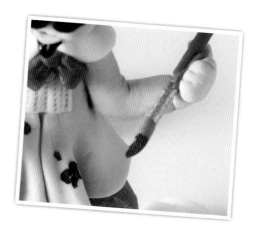

Liquid food colour is a great way to add details, such as the paint splodges on The Artist's smock and tip of his paintbrush. Do not add any water to them or they will smudge.

Brushes

For painting fine lines such as eyelashes, use a no.0000 sable paintbrush. The finer and better quality the brush, the better job you will make of it. To dust the cheeks of my figures I use a cosmetics brush, which has a sponge at one end and a brush at the other. For less detailed work, you can use a variety of sable brushes in different widths.

Food colour pens can be used to add quick and simple embellishments, such as the details on the stones in Enchanted Garden. They come in a great range of shades and are best used on hardened sugarpaste; otherwise they will mark the paste by digging into the surface.

Use a fine cosmetics brush to apply pale pink dust food colour onto the cheeks of the characters to give the faces more life. Here, I have also used a dark green dust food colour to outline the shamrock edges.

Storing sugarpaste

Sugarpaste will always store best wrapped tightly in a freezer bag. Ensure you have removed as much air as possible then place it in an airtight container to protect it from atmospheric changes. It should be kept out of the sunlight and away from any humidity, in a cool, dry area at least 50cm (20in) off the ground. If the paste has become too dry to work with, knead in some white vegetable fat (shortening). The main thing to remember with any paste is to keep it dry, cool and sealed from the air, as this will make it dry out and go hard. Freezing sugarpaste is not recommended.

Essential purchases

A visit to your local cake-decorating or sugarcraft shop is a must – not only can you buy all the necessary products there, you will also come away very inspired! These products cannot be made at home with any great ease, and therefore need to be purchased.

- **White vegetable fat (shortening)**
  This is used for softening sugarpaste so that it can be extruded through a sugar press (or garlic press) more easily to make hair, grass, fluff etc. If you find your sugarpaste has dried out a bit, knead in a little of this to make it soft and pliable again.

- **CMC (Tylose) powder**
  Carboxymethylcellulose is a synthetic and inexpensive thickening agent that is used to convert sugarpaste into modelling paste. It is also used for edible glue.

- **Rainbow Dust edible paints**
  This is a new pearlescent, edible product perfect for painting straight onto sugarpaste. It is water-soluble, available in a beautiful range of colours and gives quick and easy results.

- **Confectioners' glaze**
  This product is used to highlight the eyes, shoes or anything you want to shine on your models. It is particularly useful if you want to photograph your cake, as it will really add sparkle. Apply a thin coat and let it dry, then apply a second and even a third coat to give a really deep shine. It is best kept in a small bottle with brush on the lid – this way the brush is submerged in the glaze and doesn't go hard. If you use your paintbrush to apply it, then you will have to clean it with special glaze cleaner.

CMC (Tylose) powder, white vegetable fat, Rainbow Dust edible paints and confectioners' glaze are essential products that you will need to purchase before you begin sugarcrafting (see Suppliers).

Abbreviations and equivalents

g = grams
oz = ounces (1oz = 30g approx)
cm = centimetres (1cm = ⅜in approx)
mm = millimetres
in = inches (1in = 2.5cm approx)

ml = millilitres
tsp = teaspoon (1tsp = 5ml)
tbsp = tablespoon (1tbsp = 15ml)
fl oz = fluid ounces

Edible glue

This is the glue that holds sugarpaste pieces together, used in every project in this book. Always make sure your glue is edible before applying it to your cake.

Ingredients

- 1.25ml (¼tsp) CMC (Tylose) powder
- 30ml (2tbsp) boiled water, still warm
- A few drops of white vinegar

Method

1. Mix the CMC (Tylose) powder with the warm boiled water and leave it to stand until the powder has fully dissolved. The glue should be smooth and to a dropping consistency. If the glue thickens after a few days, add a few more drops of warm water.

2. To prevent contamination or mould, add a few drops of white vinegar.

3. Store the glue in a cool, dark place and use within one week. For a larger quantity of glue, pour one pint of cool boiled water into a blender, add one heaped teaspoonful of CMC powder and blitz for a few seconds.

TIP *To make a stronger edible glue, add an extra pinch of CMC (Tylose) to the basic recipe and mix into a stiff paste.*

UK / US terms

UK	US
CMC powder	Tylose powder
cornflour	cornstarch
cocktail stick	toothpick
icing sugar	confectioners' sugar
sugarpaste	rolled fondant icing
white vegetable fat	shortening

Modelling Cake Toppers

Mastering modelling with sugarpaste is the key to creating professional-looking cake toppers. This section reveals all the tools and techniques you need to help sharpen your modelling skills.

General equipment

There is a myriad of tools on the market for cake decorating and sugarcraft, but many of them are simply unnecessary. The following list gives my recommended essentials for making cake toppers, and these are the items that form the **basic tool kit** listed in each of the projects in this book.

- **Large non-stick rolling pin**
  For rolling out sugarpaste and marzipan.

- **Textured rolling pins (1)**
  For creating decorative patterns in paste – for example, rice textured, daisy patterned and ribbed.

- **Quality sable paintbrushes (2)**
  For painting on sugarpaste and for modelling – used mainly for painting facial features and applying edible glue. The end of a paintbrush can be pushed into models to create nostrils and to curl laces of paste around to make curly tails or hair.

- **Good-quality stainless steel cutters (3)**
  Round, square, rectangle, butterfly, heart, petal/blossom – in assorted sizes. For cutting out shapes for decoration.

- **Frilling tool**
  For making frills in sugarpaste pieces – a cocktail stick (toothpick) can be used instead.

- **Non-stick flexi mat**
  For placing over modelled parts to prevent them drying out – freezer bags can be used instead.

- **Flower former (4)**
  For placing parts, e.g. heads, in while working on them so that they do not lose their shape. A piece of swimming noodle with a hole in the middle will make a good alternative.

- **Hair gun (5)**
  A very simple tool, used to make hair, grass, wool, etc.

- **Plunger cutters (6)**
  For cutting out different shapes in sugarpaste – such as daisies, hearts, stars and flowers.

- **Wooden spacing rods (7)**
  For achieving an even thickness when rolling out sugarpaste – available in various thicknesses.

- **Cake boards (8)**
  For giving support to the finished cake – 12mm (½in) thickness is ideal.

- **Cake cards**
  For placing sugarpaste models on while working on them before transferring them to the cake.

- **Sugar press (9)**
  For extruding lengths of paste to make grass, wool, fluff and hair – a standard garlic press, found in all kitchens, is also very effective for this.

- **Paint palette (10)**
  For mixing liquid food colour or dust food colour and clear alcohol in for painting on sugarpaste.

Specific modelling tools

A whole book could be filled talking about these, as there are so many different varieties available. However, I use the white plastic set that has a number on each tool. I refer to the number on the tool throughout the book. They are inexpensive, light and easy to work with, and are available to buy from my website (see Suppliers).

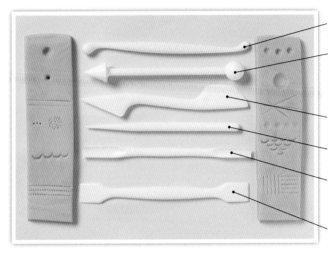

No.1: bone tool – used to put the ears on animals.

No.3: tapered cone/ball tool – the pointed end is used for hollowing out the bottom of sleeves and legs, making holes in the tops of bottles, etc.

No.4: knife tool – for cutting and marking fingers and toes.

No.5: small pointed tool – used for nostrils and making holes.

No.11: smiley tool – invaluable for marking mouths, eyelids and fish scales.

No.12: double-ended serrated tool – for adding stitch marks on teddy bears, etc.

Securing and supporting models

Sugarpaste models need to be held together in several ways. Small parts can be attached with edible glue (see Sugarpaste), but larger parts, such as heads and arms, will require additional support.

   Throughout the book I use pieces of dry spaghetti for this purpose. The spaghetti is inserted into the models – into the hip, shoulder or body, for example – onto which you can attach another piece – the leg, arm or head. Leave 2cm (¾in) showing at the top to support the head, and 1cm (⅜in) to support arms and legs.

   The pieces will still require some edible glue to bond them, but will have more support and will stay rigid. When inserting spaghetti to support heads, make sure that it is pushed into the body in a very vertical position otherwise the head will tilt backwards and become vulnerable.

   I recommend using dry raw spaghetti because it is food and is much safer than using cocktail sticks (toothpicks), which could cause harm, particularly to children. However, I would always advise that any spaghetti pieces used are removed before eating the cake and decorations.

   Sugarpaste models sometimes need to be supported with foam or cardboard while they are drying to prevent parts from flopping over or drooping down. Advice on where this may be necessary is given in the project instructions. The soft pellets used for packing are wonderful for supporting your work, especially for propping up arms and knees.

Basic shapes

There are four basic shapes required for modelling. Every character in this book begins with a ball; this shape must be rolled first, regardless of whatever shape you are trying to make.

BALL

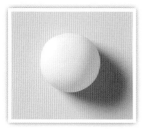

The first step is always to roll a ball to make a perfectly smooth surface with no cracks or creases.

For example:
You can indent the ball around the eye area to shape a head.

SAUSAGE

From this shape we can make arms and legs. Simply roll the ball onto the work surface and lengthen by rolling with your finger, using an even pressure to keep the thickness uniform along the length.

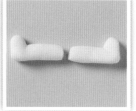

For example:
When you have rolled the sausage shape, you can then turn the rounded ends upwards to form the feet, with or without toes.

CONE

This shape forms the basis of all bodies. It is made by rolling and narrowing the ball at one end; leaving it fatter at the other end.

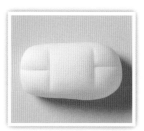

For example:
You can use the cone the opposite way to make a different body shape, or divide the widest end to make the body and legs in one piece.

OVAL

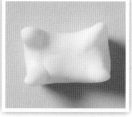

The least used of all the basic shapes, it is used to make ears, muzzles, pads and other small parts, or can be made into a body shape. It is made in the same way as the sausage, by applying even pressure to the ball, but not taking it so far.

For example:
To make the body of an animal with four legs, mark the oval shape at each end into two sections then pull out each one into a smooth rounded leg shape.

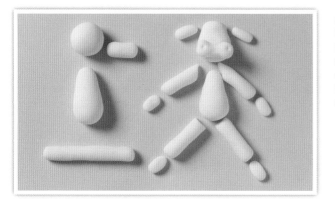

All four basic shapes were used to make this cow – a ball for the head, shaped around the eye area, an oval shape for the nose, ears and hooves, a cone for the body and a sausage shape for the arms and legs.

Pirate Pete

Arrghhh me hearties, Pirate Pete I be; a man with salt runnin' through me veins. The cutlass has been me trusty mate for many a sail and accustomed to her I've become. If you be in the mood for an adventure, step aboard and join me an' me feathered friend.

You will need:

Sugarpaste

- 107g (3¾oz) light brown
- 70g (2½oz) dark blue
- 51g (1¾oz) red
- 35g (1¼oz) flesh
- 28g (1⅛oz) lime green
- 11g (¼oz) black
- 11g (¼oz) dark brown
- 11g (¼oz) grey
- 5g (⅛oz) yellow

Materials

- 10g (¼oz) white modelling paste
- CMC (Tylose)
- Red liquid food colour
- Edible glue

Equipment

- 6cm (2½in), 4cm (1¾in), 3cm (1¼in) circle cutters
- FMM wood impression mat (optional)
- Basic tool kit (see Modelling Cake Toppers)

The pirate

THE BOOTS

1. **To make the boots** you will need 10g (¼oz) of dark brown sugarpaste with CMC (Tylose) added. Roll into a sausage shape, cut in half and turn up the ends to form the feet. Using tool no.4, mark a line around the base of each boot to form the soles and another line across for the heels (**A**).

2. **For the cuffs** around the top of each boot equally divide and roll out 1g (⅛oz) of dark brown sugarpaste to measure 1 x 5cm (⅜ x 2in). Using tool no.4, mark a section along the length of each cuff (**A**) then attach around the top of each boot. Insert a piece of dry spaghetti through the top of the boots, leaving 4cm (1½in) showing. Set aside.

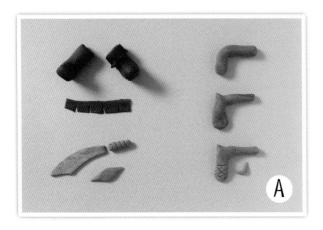

TIP *It is always a good idea to make the shoes or boots first to allow them to harden up a little in order to support the standing figure.*

THE CUTLASS AND PISTOL

1. **To complete the cutlass** you will need 5g (⅛in) of grey sugarpaste with CMC added. Roll out a piece to measure 1.5 x 5cm (⅝ x 2in) with a thickness of 5mm (¼in) and cut out the cutlass shape using tool no.4 (**A**). Roll a small sausage shape for the handle and mark lines across using tool no.4. Push a piece of dry spaghetti into the end of the handle and insert carefully through the blade to give it support. Make the sheath after the hand is in place. Take 1g (⅛oz) of grey sugarpaste, roll into a sausage shape tapered at both ends and flatten with your finger in the centre.

2. **For the pistol** add some CMC to 4g (⅛oz) of grey sugarpaste and roll into a short sausage shape. Bend the shape in half then flatten the handle at one end and mark in a crisscross design using tool no.4. Pinch out the hammer on the bend of the frame and roll the barrel to make it thinner. When you have achieved your desired shape make a straight cut at the end of the barrel and push some dry spaghetti into it to make a hole. To make the trigger, roll a very small amount of grey sugarpaste into a tapered curved sausage shape (**A**). Set aside for making the trigger cover later.

THE BODY AND LEGS

1. **For the legs** roll 44g (1⅝in) of dark blue sugarpaste into a smooth ball and then into a carrot shape. Slightly flatten the shape with your hand and, using the widest end, divide a third from the bottom for the legs. Round off the edges and keep the legs very short and fat; you may need to push the ends upwards to make them thicker (**B**).

2. Slip the boots onto the end of each leg and stand the figure upright. Push a further piece of dry spaghetti down from the top of the body through each leg and into the boots to give it extra support and push another short piece of dry spaghetti into the shoulder. Leave the figure to harden overnight before dressing.

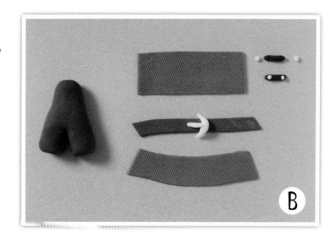

THE COAT AND BELT

1. **For the upper half of the coat** roll out 14g (½oz) of red sugarpaste and apply edible glue around the body. The strip should be long enough to reach from the back of the neck to the waist (**B**). Bring the seam together at the front and trim any excess sugarpaste from the shoulder.

2. **For the lower half of the coat** you will need 13g (⅜oz) of red sugarpaste rolled out and cut into a strip measuring 2 x 10cm (¾ x 4in) (**B**). Apply some edible glue around the waistline and attach, bringing the edges around to meet at the front.

3. **Make two fastenings** for the front of the coat using 1g (⅛oz) of black sugarpaste. Take off enough to roll two small sausage shapes measuring 1.5cm (⅝in) in length, flatten each one with your finger and attach to the front of the jacket. From 1g (⅛oz) of yellow sugarpaste, roll two tiny balls for the buttons and attach at each end (**B**). Set the leftover yellow sugarpaste aside.

4. **To make the belt** you will need 7g (¼oz) of dark blue sugarpaste rolled out and cut into a strip measuring 1 x 11cm (⅜ x 4⅝in). Drape around the waistline and cross over at the front. Roll the leftover yellow sugarpaste into a curved banana shape for the buckle and attach to the front. Roll a small yellow pin and attach over the buckle (**B**).

THE ARMS, COLLARS AND FRILLS

1. **To make the arms** you will need 18g (⅝oz) of red sugarpaste with CMC added. Roll into a sausage shape measuring 12cm (4½in) in length. Make a straight cut in the centre and bend each arm at the elbow (**C**). Keeping the rounded end at the top, slip the right arm over the spaghetti at the shoulder and rest the other end on the hip, turning the elbow out a little. Push a short piece of dry spaghetti into the wrist area.

2. Attach the left arm to the shoulder, keeping the upper half close to the body. Push a length of dry spaghetti through the wrist and arm and into the body to give it support, leaving 1cm (⅜in) showing at the wrist (**C**).

3. **To make the frills** you will need 7g (¼oz) of white modelling paste rolled out very thinly. Cut out a piece to measure 1.5 x 5cm (⅝ x 2in) for the neck frill. Turn the end under and make three folds, narrow at the top and attach to the neck of the jacket. Make two more frills for the sleeves, cutting out a piece to measure 1.5 x 10cm (⅝ x 4in). Again turn the end under and make the frill to a finished length of 4cm (1¾in) (**C**). Set aside.

4. **For the collar** roll out 3g (⅛oz) of red sugarpaste and cut a strip measuring 1.5 x 6cm (⅝ x 2½in). Make a diagonal cut at either end and attach it to the jacket, turning it over to bring the edges around to the front (**C**).

THE HANDS

1. **To make the hands** equally divide 8g (¼oz) of flesh sugarpaste, add a little CMC and roll into a fat cone shape. Mark the thumb on the same side for both and soften the edges. Indent the palm of one hand with your finger and use tool no.4 to mark the knuckles, making a straight cut at the wrist (**C**).

2. Secure the cutlass to the belt and slip the right hand over the spaghetti at the wrist, attaching it to the cutlass. Make the shield to go over the hand using a small amount from 1g (⅛oz) of grey sugarpaste. Roll into a banana shape and flatten, keeping the ends pointed. Attach over the back of the hand and connect to the cutlass. The cutlass may need to be supported until dry to keep it in place.

3. Slip the right hand over the spaghetti at the wrist and place the pistol securely into the palm. Make a separate index finger to go over the trigger area. Using the

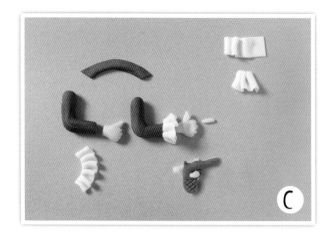

leftover grey sugarpaste, roll a small sausage shape to make the trigger shield. Fasten this over the finger and attach to the knuckles (**C**). Attach the frills over the wrist to finish.

THE HEAD

1. **To make the head and neck** you will need 25g (1oz) of flesh sugarpaste with CMC added. Roll into a ball, pull down the neck and trim the length to about 1cm (⅜in) (**D**).

2. **Make the nose** by taking off a small piece from a further 2g (⅛oz) of flesh sugarpaste and rolling into an oval shape. Attach to the centre of the face and pinch lightly in the centre (**D**). Mark the nostrils with tool no.5.

3. **To make the mouth** push the end of tool no.1 into the side of the face, making a cavity large enough to take the teeth (**D**).

4. **To make the teeth** take off a third from 1g (⅛oz) of white modelling paste, roll into an oval shape and using tool no.4, mark vertical lines and a horizontal line across the middle. Apply some edible glue inside the mouth and place the teeth inside. Use the leftover flesh sugarpaste to make a tapered cone shape for the lips. Place the pointed end at the centre top of the teeth and wrap around the bottom (**D**).

5. **To make the eye** take off a small amount of white modelling paste and roll into an oval shape. Add a dot of black sugarpaste for the pupil over the top (**D**).

6. **To make the eye patch and eyebrows** you will need 1g (⅛oz) of black sugarpaste. Shape a third of the black sugarpaste into an oval shape, flatten with your finger to form an eye patch shape and attach over the right eye. From another third, roll very thin laces to connect from each side of the patch and attach across the head. Take off another third for the eyebrows and divide equally. Roll into two short tapered cones, shape and attach in place (**D**).

7. **Shape the moustache** by equally dividing 1g (⅛oz) of black sugarpaste and rolling into two tapered cone shapes. Attach the points directly underneath the nose and bring around the sides of the mouth. Roll 3g (⅛oz) of black sugarpaste into a fat cone shape for the beard, slightly flatten with your finger and attach, following the line of the mouth (**D**). Mark the hair with tool no.4.

THE HEADSCARF AND TRI-CORNERED HAT

1. **To make the headscarf** take 3g (⅛oz) of red sugarpaste, roll out and use a cutter to take out a 4cm (1¾in) circle (**E**). Attach to the top of the head, bringing it around the forehead.

2. **For the tri-cornered hat** you will need 15g (½oz) of dark blue sugarpaste mixed together with some CMC. Roll and cut out a 6cm (2½in) circle using a cutter. Turn up the edges on three sides and pinch the corners together (**E**).

3. **To make the scull and crossbones** you will need 1g (⅛oz) of white modelling paste. Take off a third and roll into a ball then into a short sausage shape. Press out the top to widen and narrow the bottom a little to form the scull shape. Using a piece of dry spaghetti, mark two holes for the eyes and one for the nose. Insert the tip of tool no.4 and shape the hole for the nose into a trianglular shape. Using the small end of the smiley tool, mark a tiny mouth then mark the teeth with the point of tool no.4 (**E**).

4. Take a very small amount of the white modelling paste and roll two small sausage shapes. Narrow in the centre to make them very thin then use tool no.4 to indent the ends to resemble a bone (**E**). Attach in a cross shape to the front of the hat and secure the scull over the top.

The treasure chest

1. **For the treasure chest** knead one teaspoonful of CMC into 106g (3⅝oz) of light brown sugarpaste. Roll into a smooth, fat sausage then form a cube shape. Narrow at the bottom and keep the top nicely rounded (**F**). Press a FMM wood impression mat around the chest, or use tool no.4 to mark. Using the edge of a ruler, mark a line a third of the way down from the top to shape the lid.

2. **To make the trim** to go over the top of the lid you will need to roll 2g (⅛oz) of yellow sugarpaste into a strip measuring 6 x 1cm (2½ x ⅜in). Set the leftover sugarpaste aside and attach the trim to the top of the chest. Using the end of your paintbrush, indent holes down the strip and fill with small balls of leftover paste (**F**).

3. **To make the lock** you will need a small ball of the yellow sugarpaste rolled into a cone shape. Flatten with your finger and take out a round shape at the top using either a 5mm (¼in) round cutter or the end of a drinking straw. Make the hole for the key with the end of some dry spaghetti (**F**). Secure the lock to the front of the chest.

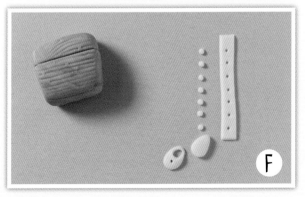

The parrot

THE BODY AND FEET

1. **Make the feet** from 2g (⅛oz) of black sugarpaste. Take off enough to make two small cone shapes and flatten with your finger. Using tool no.4, make two 'V' shapes for the claws and soften the edges (**G**). Set aside.

2. **To make the body** take 17g (⅝oz) of lime green sugarpaste, add CMC and knead. Roll into a ball and then a fat cone shape and pinch out a small tail at the back (**G**). Place on top of the chest and attach the feet underneath. Push a piece of dry spaghetti down through the centre of body and into the chest to secure, and push two short pieces of dry spaghetti into each side for the wings.

THE HEAD

1. **For the head** take 5g (⅛oz) of lime green sugarpaste and roll into a ball. Pull down the neck area by rolling the ball on the work surface and narrowing with your finger then flatten the head a little (**G**). Slip the head over the spaghetti at the top of the body and using the rounded end of tool no.4, mark lines down the lower edge of the neck to feather it. Push a short piece of dry spaghetti into the centre front of the face to hold the beak.

2. **For the beak** roll 1g (⅛oz) of light brown sugarpaste into a fat cone shape and curve the pointed end under. Slip the beak over the spaghetti. Roll a small cone shape from 1g (⅛oz) of black sugarpaste, flatten for the lower beak then attach underneath (**G**).

3. **To make the eyes** take off enough from 1g (⅛oz) of white sugarpaste to make two oval shapes and attach on either side of the head. Roll two tiny oval shapes from black sugarpaste to make the pupils and secure to the eyes. Take off a small amount of black sugarpaste and roll a very thin lace to outline the eyes and two small oval shapes to place directly underneath the eyes (**G**).

4. **Make a few more feathers** for the top of the head by taking off a small amount from 1g (⅛oz) of lime green sugarpaste to make a flattened cone shape. Using the rounded end of tool no.4, feather the shape by making downward strokes. Attach to the top of the head (**G**).

THE TAIL FEATHERS AND WINGS

1. **For the tail feathers** you will need 2g (⅛oz) of lime green sugarpaste equally divided. Roll into two cone shapes and flatten with your finger. Mark four feathers at the widest ends using tool no.4. Soften the shapes with your fingers and make a straight cut at the top. Indent a line in the centre of each feather using the rounded end of tool no.4 (**G**). Attach one set of feathers to the underside of the pinched out tail and the other set over the top.

2. **To make the wings** you will need 5g (⅛oz) of lime green sugarpaste equally divided, rolled into fat cone shapes. Indent the rounded ends with tool no.4 (**G**) and set aside.

3. **Make the blue feathers** using 2g (⅛oz) of dark blue sugarpaste equally divided. Roll into two cone shapes and flatten. Divide the ends into two, then into four. Round off each feather, marking the centres with tool no.4 and attach under the green wings (**G**). Repeat to make two more feathers using 2g (⅛oz) of yellow sugarpaste equally divided, and attach these underneath the blue feathers. Slip the completed wings over the spaghetti at the top of the body and paint some red liquid food colour around the edges.

Scooting Lammy

The ultimate two-wheelering sheep; Lammy just loves a day out riding on his scooter in the countryside, but this cool customer has taken a wrong turn and needs to consult his map. A great topper for any scooter enthusiast, Lammy brings back happy memories for young or old.

You will need:

Sugarpaste

- 49g (1¾oz) chocolate
- 35g (1¼oz) white
- 32g (1⅛oz) black
- 10g (¼oz) light brown
- 4g (⅛oz) flesh
- 2g (⅛oz) grey

Materials

- 125g (4½oz) white modelling paste
- 350g (12oz) pastillage paste
- CMC (Tylose)
- White vegetable fat (shortening)

- White edible pearl lustre paint
- Edible lustre paint in red and silver
- Light brown dust food colour
- Black paste food colour
- Icing (confectioners') sugar to dust
- Edible glue

Equipment

- 2cm (¾in),1cm (⅜in), 5mm (¼in) circle cutters
- No.26 florist wire, two 5cm (2in) lengths
- Cocktail stick (toothpick)
- Basic tool kit (see Modelling Cake Toppers)

The log

To make the log you will need 49g (1¾oz) of chocolate sugarpaste rolled into a sausage shape. Indent each end with your thumb and shape into a curve. Use tool no.4 to mark ridges in the tree to make a bark effect and dust with light brown dust food colour (**A**).

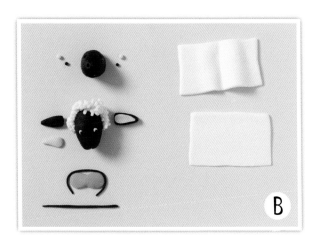

The sheep

THE BODY

1. **To make the body** roll 34g (1¼oz) of white modelling paste into a cone shape (**A**) and attach to the log. Push a piece of dry spaghetti down through the centre and into the log, leaving 2cm (¾in) showing at the top.

2. **To make the wool** for the body you will need 25g (1oz) of white sugarpaste, softened well with white vegetable fat (shortening) before filling the cup of a sugar press (or garlic press). Extrude short lengths and chop off. Apply edible glue to the whole of the body and apply the wool lengths (**A**). Push a short piece of dry spaghetti into the shoulders.

3. **Make the legs** using 8g (¼oz) of white modelling paste rolled into a thin sausage shape measuring 7cm (2¾in) in length. Make a diagonal cut in the centre and a straight cut at the end. Attach to each hip and push a short piece of dry spaghetti into the end of the legs (**A**).

4. **For the tail** take off enough from 1g (⅛oz) of white modelling paste to make a small tapered cone shape. Attach to the back, curling it at the end.

5. **To make the arms** roll 8g (¼oz) of white modelling paste into a sausage shape, make a diagonal cut in the centre and a straight cut at the end. Slip the arms over the spaghetti at the shoulders, bend at the elbows (**A**) and push a short piece of dry spaghetti into the bottom of each arm.

6. **To make the hooves** you will need 3g (⅛oz) of flesh sugarpaste with some CMC (Tylose) added to give it strength. Equally divide and make two small fat cone shapes. Using tool no.4, make a split in the hoof wide enough to slip the map inside later (**A**). Slip the hooves over the spaghetti on the legs.

THE BIKER BOOTS AND MAP

1. **For the biker boots** you will need 9g (¼oz) of light brown sugarpaste rolled into a sausage shape measuring 9cm (3½in) in length. Turn up the rounded ends to form the shoes and cut in half. Using tool no.4, mark the soles by pressing the blade around the base of each shoe (**A**). Mark the heels across at the backs.

2. Make a line down the front and top of the boots with tool no.4 then mark holes for the shoelaces using tool no.5. Roll a very thin lace from the light brown sugarpaste, cut into short pieces for the shoelaces and attach across the front of the boots (**A**). Push the boots over the spaghetti at the base of the legs then arrange the legs into position.

3. **For the map** roll out 14g (½oz) of white modelling paste to measure 3 x 6cm (1¼ x 2¼in). Lightly fold in half (**B**) and slip the side edges of the page inside the open hooves. Support with foam until dry.

THE HEAD

1. **To make the head** take 12g (⅜oz) of black sugarpaste and add a small pinch of CMC to strengthen. Roll into a cone shape and using tool no.4, mark a line down the centre front of the face then mark the mouth in a straight line at the bottom. Insert the point of tool no.10 to open the mouth in the centre and add two small holes for the nostrils. Mark two small holes for the eyes, insert a small cone of white modelling paste into each then add a tiny dot of black for the pupils (**B**). Slip the head over the spaghetti at the neck and position it so that the sheep will be looking down at the map.

2. **To make the ears** you will need 2g (⅛oz) of black sugarpaste equally divided. Roll into two small cone shapes and flatten with your finger. Take 1g (⅛oz) of flesh sugarpaste and make two smaller cone shapes to line the ears (**B**). Push a short piece of dry spaghetti into each side of the sheep's head and slip the ears over the top.

3. **For the wool** around the top and sides of the head, soften 10g (¼oz) of white sugarpaste with white vegetable fat and fill the cup of a sugar press. Extrude short lengths and chop off. Apply edible glue around the top and sides of the head and apply the wool lengths (**B**).

4. **To make the goggles** take 1g (⅛oz) of light brown sugarpaste with some CMC added and roll into a small sausage shape for the lenses. Flatten with your finger then narrow the piece in the centre so that it measures 1 x 3cm (⅜ x 1¼in) (**B**).

5. Take off enough from 1g (⅛oz) of black sugarpaste to roll a very thin lace to edge the lenses. Attach to the front of the sheep's head and roll another lace as a strap to go around the back of the head (**B**). Add a tuft more wool on top of the head to fall over the goggles.

6. **To make the spectacles**, take off two 5cm (2in) lengths from one length of No. 26 florist wire. Twist the two pieces together tightly three times in the centre to make the bridge. Insert the handle of a paintbrush in-between the wires and twist them together tightly to form a lens. Remove the brush and repeat on the other side (**C**). Trim the length of the wire and place the finished spectacles onto the head.

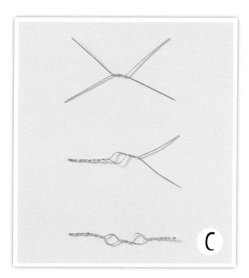

The scooter

THE MAIN FRAME

1. **To construct the scooter frame** use pastillage paste to give it strength, made from one egg white (or equivalent made up from dried egg albumen) mixed with 280g (10oz) of sifted icing (confectioners') sugar. Each piece should be left to dry for 12 hours then turned over and left for another 12 hours so that it dries out completely. It can be painted with Rainbow Dust metallic edible paint and liquid food colour and some parts can be pre-coloured with paste food colour.

TIP *Care is needed when constructing the frame of the scooter because it can break very easily.*

2. **For the back panel** take off 30g (1⅛oz) of white modelling paste and roll into a smooth ball. Flatten the ball to a thickness of 2cm (¾in), keeping its shape. Take off a third to make a straight edge at the base and press your rolling pin into the right side to make a curve. The finished piece should measure 2 x 4cm (¾ x 1½in). Reshape and trim until the dimensions are correct and set aside (**D**).

3. **To make the central frame** dust the work surface with icing sugar, roll out 30g (1⅛oz) of the pastillage paste to a thickness of 5mm (¼in) and trim to measure 14 x 3cm (5¼ x 1¼in). Measure 4cm (1½in) from the back and using a sharp knife, take off 2.5mm (⅛in) on either side to narrow the back of the frame so that the back panel will fit perfectly into this space (**D**). Make a hole right through the frame using a cocktail stick (toothpick), 2cm (¾in) from the back. Shape the frame and lay it on its side to dry for 12–24 hours.

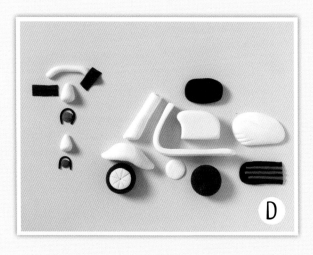
D

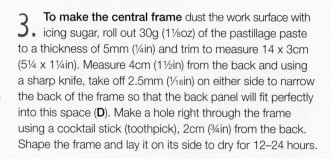
TIP *Make some extra-strong glue to fix the parts together when they are dry. Do this by adding some pastillage powder to your edible glue, making a stiff paste that can be applied with a small pallet knife or a soft brush.*

4. **Attach the back panel and frame together** using the extra-strong glue. Break a cocktail stick in half and push it into the hole at the base of the frame and into the back panel. Leave 2cm (¾in) showing underneath the frame to push into the back tyre to connect the three pieces.

THE WHEELS

1. **To make the wheels** colour 28g (1⅛oz) of pastillage with black paste food colour. Equally divide and roll into two smooth balls and flatten to a thickness of 2.5cm (1in) and a diameter of 3cm (1¼in). Indent the centre of the wheel with the end of your rolling pin (**D**).

2. **To make the wheel discs** roll out 1g (⅛oz) of white modelling paste and use a cutter to cut out four 2cm (¾in) circles. Mark a hole in each centre using tool no.3, divide the circles into eight sections using tool no.4 and attach to the centre of the tyre (**D**). Make a hole into the centre top of the tyre so that the cocktail stick on the frame can be inserted.

THE SIDE PANELS, SEAT, MUDGUARD AND FOOTMAT

1. **For the side panels** you will need 26g (1oz) of white modelling paste equally divided and shaped into two soft cone shapes. Flatten with your hands and mould into the correct shape to fit the back panel. Mark three vents on the side using tool no.4 and attach to the back panel when dry (**D**).

2. **For the seat** roll 8g (¼oz) of black sugarpaste into a short oval shape. Flatten the shape using the rolling pin to widen, turn up the end for the back (**D**) and set aside.

3. **To make the front mudguard** shape 14g (½oz) of white pastillage into an oval shape then hollow it out inside until it is wide enough to fit the wheel inside (**D**). Set aside to dry.

4. **For the foot mat** take 8g (¼oz) of black sugarpaste and roll into a short sausage shape measuring 4cm (1¾in) in length. Flatten with your rolling pin and make a straight cut at the back (**D**). Roll out 1g (⅛oz) of grey sugarpaste and cut out three thin strips to attach to the top of the mat. Secure the mat to the floor of the frame.

THE FRONT COLUMN, HANDLEBARS AND HEADLIGHTS

1. **For the front column** you will need 10g (¼oz) of white pastillage rolled into a sausage shape measuring 6cm (2½in) in length (**D**). Taper the base so that it fits snugly over the top of the front mudguard and set aside to dry.

2. **For the handlebars** roll a sausage shape from 2g (⅛oz) of white pastillage to measure 5cm (2in) in length (**D**). Shape over the top of the frame and set aside to dry.

3. **Make the hand grips** using 1g (⅛oz) of black sugarpaste rolled out thinly and cut into a strip measuring 1 x 2.5cm (⅜ x 1in). Using tool no.4 mark lines diagonally across, equally divide and attach to the ends of the handlebars (**D**). Set aside any leftover black sugarpaste to trim the headlights.

4. **For the main headlight** roll 3g (⅛oz) of white modelling paste into a small fat cone shape and flatten the front with your finger. Using cutters, cut out a 1cm (⅜in) circle for the main light and a 5mm (¼in) circle for the smaller light on the mudguard from 1g (⅛oz) of grey sugarpaste. Trim with a very thin lace of leftover black sugarpaste (**D**).

TIP *It is very important that you allow the pastillage to dry thoroughly before putting it together, otherwise it will break.*

ASSEMBLING THE SCOOTER

1. Attach the back panel to the frame, inserting cocktail sticks into the holes. Slip the back tyre over the cocktail stick and secure to the frame. Add the side panels to the back panel then attach the seat.

2. Secure the front mudguard to the front of the frame. Insert the front tyre into the mudguard and align with the back tyre then attach the front column to the frame and front mudguard. Add the handlebars to the top of the frame and place the lights into position.

3. Paint the frame, back panel, main light and front mudguard with white edible pearl lustre paint. Paint the front column, small light and side panels with red edible lustre paint and the wheel discs with sliver edible lustre paint.

Red Racer

Whether young or old, this fun racing car is sure to appeal to boys of all ages. When the flag goes up, you can almost hear the engines revving, the tyres spinning and the crowd roaring with cheers. This happy racer is guaranteed to get pole position at any celebration.

You will need:

Sugarpaste
- 210g (7¼oz) black
- 140g (5oz) red
- 11g (¼oz) grey
- 10g (¼oz) white

Materials
- 19g (¾oz) white modelling paste
- CMC (Tylose)
- Confectioners' glaze
- Rainbow Dust edible silver metallic paint
- Edible glue

Equipment
- 5mm (¼in), 6mm (¼in), 10mm (⅜in), 13mm (½in), 15mm (⅝in), 2cm (¾in), 3cm (1⅛in) circle cutters
- 6mm (¼in) square cutter
- Rainbow Dust edible silver metallic paint
- Basic tool kit (see Modelling Cake Toppers)

The car

THE BASE AND BODY

1. **To make the base** you will need 45g (1⅝oz) of red sugarpaste mixed with a good pinch of CMC (Tylose) to stiffen. Knead the paste well then roll into a sausage shape. Flatten each end of the sausage and press to create a well in the centre deep enough to take the body of the car (**A**).

2. **To make the body shape** add half a teaspoonful of CMC to 75g (2¾oz) of red sugarpaste, knead well and roll into a ball. Roll into a fat sausage shape, flattening one end for the front of the car and shaping it (**A**). Ensure that the front end is deep enough to allow you to insert a big smile.

3. Narrow the sausage shape in the centre, making a ridge along the top of the car. The finished length should be 10cm (4in). Using tool no.3, make a well in the top for the cockpit (**A**). Mark the curved lines around the side of the car using the rounded end of tool no.4.

4. **Add a large smile** at the front of the car using the edge of a 3cm (1⅛in) circle cutter. Open the smile further using the soft end of a paintbrush and roll a tiny banana shape of white modelling paste for the teeth (**A**). Apply some edible glue to the smile and attach the teeth to the mouth indent.

5. **Attach the car body** over the base and secure with edible glue.

6. **For the curved black lines** around the sides of the car, make a thin lace using 3g (⅛oz) of black sugarpaste. Ensure the lines meet neatly at the back of the car and set the leftover paste aside.

TIP *A cake smoother is a handy tool to help you roll an even lace.*

THE HEADLIGHTS

1. **For the headlights** you will need 4g (⅛oz) of red sugarpaste equally divided and rolled into two fat cone shapes. Flatten the front of the shapes with your finger (**A**).

2. **To make the eyes** thinly roll out 1g (⅛oz) of white modelling paste and use a cutter to make two 13mm (½in) circles. Repeat with the leftover black sugarpaste and smaller cutter to create two 5mm (¼in) circles. Secure the white circles to the lights and add the black circles centrally in place. Using 1g (⅛oz) of black sugarpaste, take off enough to roll out a thin lace to outline the lights and set aside (**A**).

THE DRIVER

1. **For the driver** equally divide 3g (⅛oz) of red sugarpaste then use one half to roll a small sausage shape for the body and insert inside the cockpit. Push a short piece of dry spaghetti into the top of the body. Use the remaining red sugarpaste to roll a ball for the helmet and secure in place onto the dry spaghetti (**A**).

2. **Make the headrest** using 2g (⅛oz) of red sugarpaste rolled into an oval shape and flattened. Make a straight cut at the base then push a short piece of dry spaghetti into the back of the cockpit and slip the headrest over the top. Make an insert for the back of the headrest from the remaining leftover black sugarpaste by rolling a small oval shape and flattening, making a straight cut at the base and attaching with edible glue (**A**).

3. **For the visor and windscreen** you will need to mix together 25g (1oz) of black sugarpaste with 9g (¼oz) of white modelling paste to create a mixed grey paste. Using tool no.4, cut out a tiny rectangular shape for the visor and attach to the front of the helmet. For the windscreen, use a cutter to cut out a 1.5cm (⅝in) circle from the mixed grey paste then cut off the bottom third of the circle (**A**) and place into position in front of the driver. Set aside the remaining grey paste to use for making the hubcaps later.

4. From 2g (⅛oz) of black sugarpaste, roll out a very thin lace and outline the shape of the car as shown in the main picture. Outline the headlights in the same way.

THE WHEELS

1. **To make four wheels** you will need 78g (2¾oz) of black sugarpaste mixed with half a teaspoonful of CMC. Take off 34g (1¼oz) for the larger back tyres, divide equally then roll into two balls and flatten with your fingers (**B**). Divide the remaining paste equally and repeat for the front tyres.

2. **For the hubcaps** you will need 25g (1oz) of black sugarpaste mixed together with 9g (¼oz) of white modelling paste. Roll out very thinly and use cutters to cut out two 2cm (¾in), two 1.5cm (⅝in) and four 6mm (¼in) circles. Attach the two 2cm (¾in) circles to the back tyres and the two 1.5cm (⅝in) circles to the front tyres then add a 6mm (¼in) circle in the centre of all four wheels for the hubcaps (**B**). Secure the wheels to the front and back of the car then attach the headlights and the spoiler.

THE SPOILER

1. **For the two supports** add a good pinch of CMC to 10g (¼oz) of red sugarpaste and knead well. Roll out to a 5mm (¼in) thickness and cut out two 3 x 0.5cm (1¼ x ¼in) strips (**A**). Push a piece of dry spaghetti through the centre of each strip, with 2cm (¾in) showing at the base.

2. **For the top of the spoiler** roll the red sugarpaste out to a 3mm (⅛in) thickness and roll out a sausage shape measuring 1.3 x 7cm (½ x 2¾in). Using a 6mm (¼in) square cutter, cut out a square at each end of the strip (**A**). Carefully push the upright pieces through the squares to assemble the spoiler and secure with edible glue. Equally divide 8g (¼oz) of red sugarpaste and form two cube shapes. Attach to the bottom of the supports then set aside.

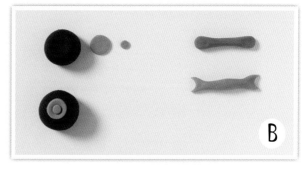

B

TIP *Make the black trims extra shiny by painting them with two coats of confectioners' glaze, letting them dry between applications.*

The wheel stack and spanner

THE WHEEL STACK

For the wheel stack make three more tyres as described for the wheels, using 60g (2¼oz) of black sugarpaste divided into three and 8g (¼oz) of grey sugarpaste to make the hubcaps (**B**).

THE SPANNER

To make the spanner roll out 3g (⅛oz) of grey sugarpaste with CMC added into a sausage shape (**B**). Narrow the shape in the centre, leaving each end a little thicker. Press the ends to flatten slightly and take out the centres using a 1cm (⅜in) circle cutter.

The flag

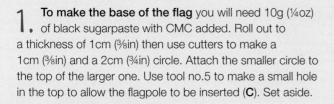

THE BASE AND FLAGPOLE

1. **To make the base of the flag** you will need 10g (¼oz) of black sugarpaste with CMC added. Roll out to a thickness of 1cm (⅜in) then use cutters to make a 1cm (⅜in) and a 2cm (¾in) circle. Attach the smaller circle to the top of the larger one. Use tool no.5 to make a small hole in the top to allow the flagpole to be inserted (**C**). Set aside.

2. **To make the flagpole** roll out 2g (⅛oz) of black sugarpaste and cut to measure approximately 6 x 1cm (2½ x ⅜in). Run a line of edible glue down the centre, place a length of dry spaghetti over the top then fold over the paste to enclose the spaghetti (**C**). Trim off the excess paste close to the spaghetti then roll it on the worktop to reduce the thickness, removing any excess paste. Set aside.

THE CHEQUERED FLAG

1. **For the flag** evenly roll out 10g (¼oz) of white sugarpaste and cut out a rectangle measuring 4 x 2.5cm (1½ x 1in). Roll out the rest of the white sugarpaste very thinly and use the square cutter to make twelve 6mm (¼in) squares. Roll out 4g (⅛oz) of black sugarpaste and cut out twelve 6mm (¼in) squares. Apply some edible glue to the flag and position the squares in an alternate pattern as shown (**C**).

> **TIP** *While the paste is soft, gently curve the edges of the flag to add dimension and give the impression of movement.*

C

2. To attach the completed flag to the flagpole apply some glue to the pole and wrap the edge of the flag around it. Allow to dry then push the pole into the base to complete.

Mum's Little Helper

This cheeky little chap is having a fantastic time helping his mum to bake his favourite chocolate cupcakes. Like any young boy he adores chocolate and loves to make a mess! This gorgeous little character will raise a smile at any occasion.

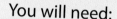

You will need:

Sugarpaste

- 50g (1¾oz) flesh
- 35g (1¼oz) yellow
- 32g (1⅛oz) orange
- 25g (1oz) teddy bear brown
- 16g (½oz) lime green
- 15g (½oz) jade green
- 8g (¼oz) chocolate
- 1g (⅛oz) dark blue

Materials

- 104g (3½oz) white modelling paste
- White vegetable fat (shortening)
- Edible glue

Equipment

- 2cm (¾in), 1cm (⅜in) circle cutters
- 2cm (¾in) square cutter
- Small blossom cutter
- Basic tool kit (see Modelling Cake Toppers)

The little boy

THE BODY AND LEGS

1. **To make the body** you will need to mix 25g (1oz) of yellow sugarpaste with 25g (1oz) of white modelling paste, kneading it together to make a smooth paste. Roll into a ball then into a cone shape (**A**). Place the body onto a card and push a piece of dry spaghetti down through the centre, leaving 2cm (¾in) showing at the top to take the head.

2. **For the legs** you will need to mix 15g (½oz) of flesh sugarpaste with 15g (½oz) of white modelling paste. Roll into a sausage shape measuring 16cm (6¼in) in length and make a straight cut in the centre. Shape the legs by narrowing them at the ankles and behind the knees (**A**). Push a short piece of dry spaghetti into the base of each leg to take the shoes.

3. **To make the trouser legs** roll out 10g (¼oz) of yellow sugarpaste into a rectangular shape measuring 3 x 6cm (1¼ x 2½in). Attach around the top of the leg with

the seam around the underneath. Make a diagonal cut at the top, attach to the body at the hip and repeat (**A**).

4. **For the shoes** you will need 9g (¼oz) of jade green sugarpaste equally divided. Roll first into balls and then into oval shapes. Make the soles using 3g (⅛oz) of white modelling paste equally divided and rolled into sausage shapes (**A**). Flatten out with your finger and secure to the shoes. Mark the heel across each shoe using tool no.4 and secure the shoes over the spaghetti at the ankles.

5. **Make the sock tops** by rolling out 4g (⅛oz) of white modelling paste and cutting into two strips measuring 2.5 x 4.5cm (1 x 1¾in). Turn over the top edge to form a cuff and attach around the ankles (**A**).

> **TIP** *Position the legs as you require at this stage before they dry out, remembering to leave enough space for the mixing bowl.*

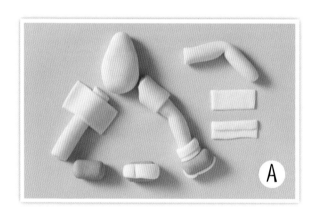

THE T-SHIRT AND ARMS

1. **To make the T-shirt** you will need 24g (1oz) of orange sugarpaste rolled out and cut into two rectangular shapes, each measuring 5 x 7cm (2 x 2¾in) (**B**). Apply some edible glue to the front of the body and place on the first rectangle. Make a straight seam at each side using tool no.4 and remove any excess. Attach the second square to the back and remove any excess where it overlaps at the side to create two perfectly fitting side seams.

2. **To make the stripes** for the front, thinly roll out 3g (⅛oz) of jade green sugarpaste. Cut a strip long enough to go across the front and a narrower one to go over the top (**B**). Using circle cutters, cut out a 2cm (¾in) circle then take out a 1cm (⅜in) circle from the centre. Slip this centrally over the spaghetti at the neck.

3. **For the arms** you will need to mix 20g (¾oz) of flesh sugarpaste with 20g (¾oz) of white modelling paste. Roll into a sausage shape and make a diagonal cut in the centre. Using the rounded ends for the hands, narrow at the wrists and inside the elbows. Flatten the palms and cut out the thumbs using tool no.4 (**B**).

4. The left hand has no visible fingers. Simply mark four lines for the knuckles using tool no.4 and remove any edges by rounding off the thumb. The right hand shows a thumb and four fingers. Mark the thumb with tool no.4 and round it off then divide the palm into four equal fingers and roll each one to make them rounded (**B**).

5. **For the T-shirt sleeves** roll out 8g (¼oz) of orange sugarpaste and cut into two strips measuring 3 x 5cm (1¼ x 2in) (**B**). Apply some edible glue to the top of each arm and place a strip over the top, making sure that the seam is underneath and out of sight. Make a diagonal cut at the top and attach to the shoulders. The left arm will need some support to lift it, and you can do this using a small piece of sponge. The right arm will rest on the leg.

6. Roll out a further 3g (⅛in) of jade green sugarpaste and cut two thick strips. Attach at the top of each sleeve to decorate them (**B**).

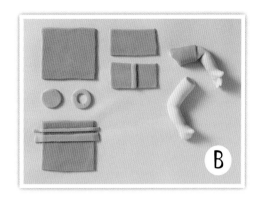

THE HEAD

1. **For the head** you will need to mix together 15g (½oz) of white modelling paste with 15g (1½oz) of flesh sugarpaste. Roll into a smooth ball then pull down the neck area from underneath, gently twisting it as you do so and forming a chin at the same time. Place the head into your hand and indent the eye area with the side of your little finger. Pull down the chin a little with your thumb (**C**). Make a straight cut at the neck and place into a flower former.

2. **Make the ears, eyes and nose** using the leftover flesh sugarpaste. Roll a small oval shape for the nose and place in the centre of the face. Use tool no.11 to mark a smile shape then turn the tool over the other way and mark again to form a circular mouth. Take the end of your paintbrush and push it into the centre of the circle, pressing it down a little to form the tongue (**C**). Using the rounded end of tool no.4, mark the lines on either side of the face.

3. **To make the teeth** roll a tiny amount of white modelling paste into a banana shape (**C**). Use tool no.4 to mark in the centre to divide the teeth. Apply some edible glue to the top lip and position the teeth in place.

4. **For the eyes** you will need a very small amount of the leftover flesh sugarpaste rolled into two tiny cone shaped eyelids. Using the end of your paintbrush, push the eyelid upwards in the centre to leave a space for the eye. Using a tiny amount of dark blue sugarpaste, roll two balls and insert into the space. Outline the eyes with a very thin lace of dark brown sugarpaste (**C**) and attach in place.

5. **Make the ears** by rolling a small amount of flesh sugarpaste into two cone shapes. Attach to the sides of the head, with the top of the ears parallel to the centre of the eyes (**C**).

6. **For the hair** soften 10g (¼oz) of teddy bear brown sugarpaste with some white vegetable fat (shortening), and fill the cup of a sugar press (or garlic press). Gently extrude short strands and cut them off with tool no.4. Apply edible glue around the head and begin to style the hair, starting at the top and sides then working your way around the back until it is complete (**C**).

7. Attach the head to the top of the body by slipping over the spaghetti at the neck.

TIP *If you don't have a flower former, you can use a piece of swimming noodle with a hole in the centre.*

The mixing bowl and spoon

THE WOODEN SPOON

For the wooden spoon you will need to mix 1g (⅛oz) of blue sugarpaste with 1g (⅛oz) of modelling paste. Roll into a ball then use your fingers to make an elongated cone shape. Flatten the widest end to form the bowl of the spoon and continue to roll the rest of the paste to make it thinner for the handle. Trim off at the top if it becomes too long. Push a piece of dry spaghetti through the handle to the bowl to keep it straight (**D**) and set the spoon aside.

THE MIXING BOWL

1. **For the mixing bowl** you will need to mix 15g (½oz) of teddy bear brown sugarpaste with 15g (½oz) of modelling paste. Roll into a ball then slice off one side to form the top of the bowl and hollow out slightly using tool no.3. Use tool no.4 to mark around the edge to make a ridge and mark two more vertical lines down the front of the bowl (**D**).

2. Attach the wooden spoon to the left hand of the boy, and secure it to the top of the mixing bowl.

3. **Make the chocolate mixture** using 8g (¼oz) of chocolate sugarpaste mixed with white vegetable fat to make it very soft. Apply some edible glue to the top of the bowl and around the spoon and add the chocolate mixture in irregular shapes, giving it some texture with the end of your paintbrush or tool no.1 (**D**). Add some spatters of chocolate to the face, hands and T-shirt.

The recipe book

1. **To make the cover** roll out 16g (½oz) of lime green sugarpaste and cut out a strip measuring 2.5 x 6cm (1 x 2½in) (**E**).

2. **To make the pages** you will need 6g (⅛oz) of white modelling paste rolled out thinly. Using a 2cm (¾in) square cutter, cut out five pages and attach them together on the right side of the strip (**E**).

3. Fold over the rest of the cover to form the book and use tool no.4 to mark the spine on the fold. Mark the centre of the cover with a small blossom cutter and place the book beside the little boy.

Lucky Leprechaun

This charming leprechaun is arriving in grand style, riding a majestic white unicorn and carrying a beautiful bunch of roses to impress his lady on her special day. This magical topper will be the ultimate lucky charm at any occasion.

You will need:

Sugarpaste
- 35g (1¼oz) duck egg blue
- 32g (1⅛oz) jade green
- 23g (⅞oz) flesh
- 14g (½oz) light brown
- 2g (⅛oz) pale pink
- 1g (⅛oz) dark brown
- 1g (⅛oz) black

Equipment
- Basic tool kit (see Modelling Cake Toppers)

Materials
- 164g (5¾oz) white modelling paste
- Dust food colour in pink and dark brown
- Rainbow Dust edible gold paint
- White vegetable fat (shortening)
- CMC (Tylose)
- Edible glue

The unicorn

THE BODY

1. **To make the body** you will need 80g (2⅞oz) of white modelling paste. Roll into a ball then into a fat sausage shape. Pull up the neck and shape the chest (**A**).

2. **Shape the back leg** by rolling 9g (¼oz) of white modelling paste into a ball then narrowing half of the ball to lengthen the lower leg. Indent the hoof at the narrow end using tool no.4, bend the leg and attach to the rear side of the body (**A**).

3. **For the front legs** equally divide 18g (⅝oz) of white modelling paste into the same shape as the back leg, bending in the opposite direction. Attach to each side of the unicorn (**A**). Paint the hooves with edible gold paint and a soft brush.

4. **For the tail** soften 10g (¼oz) of white modelling paste with white vegetable fat (shortening) and fill the cup of a sugar press (or garlic press). Extrude the hair into long lengths for the tail. Cut off using tool no.4 and attach to the back of the horse, curling the tail towards the back (**A**).

THE HEAD

1. **For the head** you will need 21g (¾oz) of white modelling paste rolled into a ball. Narrow half of the ball to shape the front of the muzzle. Indent the nostrils with the end of your paintbrush, making the holes quite large (**B**).

2. **To make the eyes** mark two small holes for the eye sockets with tool no.5 and using 1g (⅛oz) of dark brown sugarpaste, make two small cone shapes to fill the eye socket holes. Outline the eyes with a thin lace taken from 1g (⅛oz) of black sugarpaste (**B**).

3. **For the ears** roll two small cone shapes from 1g (⅛oz) of white modelling paste, flatten with your finger and make a straight cut at the widest end (**B**). Attach to the top of the head.

4. **Make a lower lip** by rolling a smaller flattened cone shape and attaching under the front jaw (**B**). Dust the inside of the nostrils and ears with pink dust food colour and around the nose with dark brown dust food colour.

5. **To make the horn** push a hole in the forehead with some dry spaghetti. You will need 3g (⅛oz) of light brown sugarpaste with CMC (Tylose) added. Roll into a tapered sausage shape and push a piece of dry spaghetti through the centre to keep it upright, leaving 2cm (¾in) showing at the base. Mark the twisted pattern using tool no.4 (**B**) and push the horn into the head. Slip the head over the spaghetti at the neck. Paint the horn using edible gold paint and a soft brush.

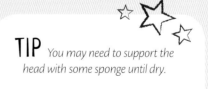

TIP *You may need to support the head with some sponge until dry.*

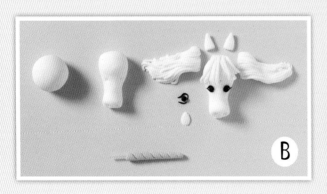

6. **For the mane** soften 25g (1oz) of white modelling paste with white vegetable fat, fill the cup of a sugar press and extrude some long hair. Allow the mane to fall on either side, down the back of the neck and around the horn (**B**).

The leprechaun

THE BOOTS

Make two small boots using 4g (⅛oz) of jade green sugarpaste equally divided. Roll each piece into a cone shape and turn up the points for the front of each boot. Push up the back of the cone and insert the point of tool no.3 into the top to hollow out. Mark the heels across the backs with tool no.4 (**C**). Set aside.

THE BODY

1. **To make the body and legs** you will need 20g (¾oz) of duck egg blue sugarpaste. Add a good pinch of CMC and roll into a carrot shape. Smooth the carrot shape to flatten slightly then place the point of tool no.4 in the centre, dividing the wider, lower half into two for the legs (**C**). Soften all the edges to make the legs smooth and round.

2. Bend the legs at the knee, adjusting the length if necessary. Make a straight cut at the base of the leg and push a short piece of dry spaghetti into the end. Place the body on top of the unicorn, pushing a piece of dry spaghetti down through the centre of the leprechaun and into the unicorn's body to give it support. Push a short piece of dry spaghetti into the shoulders. Slip the boots over the spaghetti at the ankles.

3. **For the skirt** roll out 5g (⅛oz) of duck egg blue sugarpaste and cut into a 8 x 15cm (3¼ x 6in) strip. Using tool no.4, divide into sections along one edge. Add some stitch marks using tool no.12 (**C**). Attach the skirt around the waist of the rider, making a join at the back.

4. **To make the belt** roll out 3g (⅛oz) of jade green sugarpaste and cut a narrow strip measuring 9cm (3½in) in length (**C**). Attach around the waist and then cross over at the side.

5. **For the arms** you will need 10g (¼oz) of duck egg blue sugarpaste rolled into a sausage shape. Cut the shape in half, using the rounded ends for the tops and the straight edges for the wrists. Bend the arms at the elbows (**C**) and attach over the spaghetti at the top of the body. Push a short piece of dry spaghetti into each wrist.

THE HEAD AND HANDS

1. **To make the head and hands** you will need 23g (⅞oz) of flesh sugarpaste with CMC added. Take off 3g (⅛oz) for the hands and divide equally. Roll into two small cone shapes, flattening slightly with your finger. Mark the thumbs with tool no.4 and remove the edges to make them round. Mark the knuckles by indenting three lines across the top using tool no.4. Make a straight cut at the wrist and slip over the spaghetti at the end of the arm (**D**).

2. **For the head** roll the remainder of the flesh sugarpaste into a ball. Pull down a neck from underneath and make a chin as you do so. Indent the eye area, removing any sharp lines (**D**). Make a straight cut at the neck and use the leftover sugarpaste to create the ears and nose.

THE HAT AND CLOAK

1. **For the hat** roll 3g (⅛oz) of jade green sugarpaste into a ball and flatten into an oval shape for the brim. Roll 2g (⅛oz) of jade green sugarpaste into an oval shape and attach to the top of the hat (**D**). Indent with the handle of your paintbrush. Push a short piece of dry spaghetti into the top of the head and slip the hat over the top, securing with edible glue.

2. **For the cloak** you will need 20g (¾oz) of jade green sugarpaste rolled into a sausage shape measuring 7cm (2¾in) in length. Use a rolling pin to roll out the sausage shape to a width of 7cm (2¾in) (**E**). Make a straight cut at the top and mark the collar with two diagonal cuts, trimming any excess paste away. Attach to the back of the rider and over the back of the horse. From 1g (⅛oz) of light brown sugarpaste, take off enough to roll a thin lace to fasten the cloak at the front.

3. **Create the facial features** by first rolling a small cone shape for the nose and attaching to the centre of the face. Mark a smile using tool no.11 and use the soft end of your paintbrush to slightly open the mouth. Make two small holes for the eye sockets using tool no.5 and roll two tiny cone shapes from white modelling paste to fill. Add two very small balls of dark brown sugarpaste over the top for the pupils. Outline the eyes by rolling a very fine dark brown sugarpaste lace and placing it over and underneath them (**D**).

4. **For the ears** use the leftover flesh sugarpaste to make two tiny cone shapes. Flatten them slightly and attach to the sides of the head, making a point at the top of each ear. Indent with the end of your paintbrush to secure (**D**).

5. **For the hair** apply a coat of edible glue over the head and fill the cup of the sugar press with 10g (¼oz) of light brown sugarpaste (without CMC) softened with white vegetable fat (**D**). Extrude a few strands of hair and apply in a thin layer around the head. Add a few strands over the forehead.

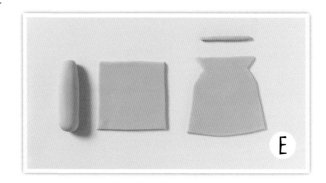

The roses

1. **To make the roses and ribbon** you will need 2g (⅛oz) of pale pink sugarpaste. Take off a small amount and roll into a thin sausage shape then use the rolling pin to thin out one edge. Curl the end over onto the strip two or three times and break off the remaining paste (**F**). Narrow the base of the flower that you have formed and open out the petals with your finger. Repeat to create three roses.

2. **To make a ribbon** roll a thin lace of the pale pink sugarpaste and hang this over the hand of the rider (**F**). Attach the three roses securely to the top.

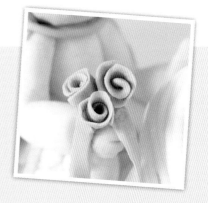

Alligator Antics

A proud mother alligator sits beside her nest brimming with eggs and joyfully welcomes her first baby into the world. The snappy little one rests in his half-shattered eggshell, gazing around in wonder at his surroundings. A lovely little topper to celebrate any new arrival!

You will need:

Sugarpaste

- 135g (4¾oz) green
- 24g (1oz) lime green
- 23g (1oz) pastel green
- 12g (⅜oz) dark brown
- 10g (¼oz) light brown
- 5g (⅛oz) fuchsia pink
- 4g (⅛oz) white
- 2g (⅛oz) yellow
- 2g (⅛oz) black

Materials

- 18g (¾oz) white modelling paste
- White vegetable fat (shortening)
- CMC (Tylose)
- Paste food colour in olive green and white
- Green dust food colour
- Edible glue

Equipment

- 4cm (1½in) circle cutter
- Scissors
- Basic tool kit (see Modelling Cake Toppers)

The mother alligator

THE BODY AND TAIL

1. **To create the body and tail** you will need 65g (2⅜oz) of green sugarpaste with CMC (Tylose) added. Roll the paste into a cone shape, giving it plenty of height and pull out the tail at the back of the cone. Shape the tail so that it tapers towards the end then make a soft curve to create a sense of movement (**A**). Pinch with your fingers at the top of the tail, making a ridge all the way along. Push a length of dry spaghetti down through the centre of the body, leaving 2cm (¾in) showing at the top.

2. Add some olive green paste food colour to 2g (⅛oz) of white modelling paste and roll out very thinly. Cut a strip measuring 1 x 12cm (⅜ x 4½in) and cut out some triangular shapes using tool no.4 (**A**). Apply a line of edible glue down the back and tail of the alligator and attach the triangular shapes edge to edge in a straight line.

3. **To make the alligator's chest** you will need 12g (⅜oz) of lime green sugarpaste rolled into a flattened cone shape. Attach to the front of the body and make horizontal lines across using tool no.4 (**A**).

THE LEGS

1. **For the back legs** you will need 43g (1⅝oz) of green sugarpaste equally divided. Roll each piece into a ball then lengthen half of each ball by rolling the shape on the work surface, keeping the thigh nicely rounded. Turn up the foot at the narrow end and shape as shown (**A**). Make two 'V' shapes along the top of the foot with tool no.4 to mark out the toes then soften with your fingers to remove the edges. Push a piece of dry spaghetti into the hipline of the body and attach the leg.

2. **For the front legs** push a piece of dry spaghetti a third of the way down the alligator's body cone and out from the sides for support. You will need 8g (¼oz) of green sugarpaste equally divided and rolled into a fat cone shape. Slip the narrower end over the spaghetti at the side of the body and support if necessary until dry. Mark the end of the leg with tool no.4.

3. **To make the yellow markings** take off small amounts from 2g (⅛oz) of yellow sugarpaste, form them into irregular shapes with your fingers and apply to the legs. Use the remaining yellow sugarpaste to make little oval shapes for the nails (**A**).

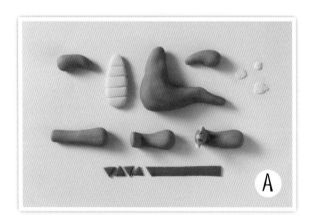

TIP *Let the body harden a little before you attach the head. This will help the alligator to stand upright..*

THE HEAD

1. **To make the head** roll 18g (⅝oz) of green sugarpaste into a short cone shape, slightly flattening it to broaden it at the top (**B**). Add two small balls of green sugarpaste to the front of the nose and indent with the end of your paintbrush to make two holes for the nostrils. Mark horizontal lines across the front of the face with tool no.4.

2. **For the lower jaw** roll 6g (⅛oz) of lime green sugarpaste into a flattened cone shape then indent the centre for the tongue to sit in. To make the tongue roll 2g (⅛oz) of fuchsia sugarpaste into a tapered cone shape (**B**). Flatten with your finger and attach inside the lower jaw. Secure the head to the lower jaw, keeping it open so that the tongue is visible.

3. **For the eyes** roll two small balls from 1g (⅛oz) of white sugarpaste and add a tiny pupil from 1g (⅛oz) of black sugarpaste, directing the eyes as you require. Outline the top of each eye with a tiny lace made from 1g (⅛oz) of green sugarpaste and set aside the leftover paste (**B**).

4. **Make two cheeks** from 6g (⅛oz) of lime green sugarpaste, equally divided and rolled into two small, flattened balls (**B**). Attach to each side of the head.

5. **Form the hair** from the leftover green sugarpaste by rolling three tapered cone shapes. Pinch them together at the bottom and secure to the top of the head (**B**).

6. **To make the bow** you will need 3g (⅛oz) of fuchsia sugarpaste. Make two small, flattened cone shapes and indent the sides to shape. Place one on either side of the hair, add a small round ball in the centre then use tool no.4 to mark lines from the centre of the bow outwards (**B**).

The baby alligator

THE BROKEN EGGSHELL

To make the broken eggshell roll 10g (¼oz) of white modelling paste into a smooth ball and place on the end of a rolling pin. Hollow out the shape, pulling down the edges with your fingers, so that the egg is approximately 4cm (1½in) in height. Using a small pair of scissors, make some 'V' shaped cuts in the edges of the egg to create the appearance of a broken shell (**C**). Set any leftover paste aside.

TIP *The cavity at the top of the eggshell should be 4cm (1½in) wide in order to fit the baby alligator inside.*

THE BABY ALLIGATOR'S BODY

1. **To make the body** you will need 12g (⅜oz) of pastel green sugarpaste mixed with CMC and rolled into a cone shape (**C**). Push a piece of dry spaghetti down through the centre, leaving 2cm (¾in) showing at the top to support the head.

2. **For the front legs** take 4g (⅛oz) of pastel green sugarpaste and divide equally. Roll into two fat cone shapes and indent the paw marks at the fat ends using tool no.4 (**C**). Push a short piece of dry spaghetti into the sides of the body and slip the arms over the top.

3. **For the chest** you will need 2g (⅛oz) of white sugarpaste mixed with 1g (⅛oz) of pastel green sugarpaste to make a lighter shade. Take off 2g (⅛oz) of the mixed paste and roll into a small cone shape, flattening with your finger to shape it to fit down the front of the body (**C**). Mark horizontal lines across the chest using tool no.4.

THE BABY ALLIGATOR'S HEAD

1. **To make the head** you will need 6g (⅛oz) of pastel green sugarpaste with CMC added, rolled into a short flattened cone shape (**C**). Mark the mouth with the edge of a circle cutter then indent the nostrils using tool no.5. Mark some lines down the snout with tool no.4.

2. **Make the cheeks** using the leftover mixed green paste from the chest. Roll into two tapered cone shapes and attach to the sides of the head (**C**). Slip the head over the spaghetti at the top of the body to secure in place.

3. **For the eyes** roll two small round balls using the leftover paste from the broken eggshell and position on the head. Take off enough from 1g (⅛oz) of black sugarpaste to make the pupils and attach. Make two tiny laces from pastel green sugarpaste and outline each eye (**C**).

4. Place 1g (⅛oz) of white sugarpaste into the bottom of the eggshell and secure the baby alligator inside.

TIP *Use a soft brush to carefully dab dark green dust food colour over the head and paws of the baby alligator. Highlight the eyes using a cocktail stick (toothpick) dipped into some white paste food colour.*

The nest and eggs

THE NEST

To complete the nest you will need 10g (¼oz) of light brown sugarpaste mixed roughly together with 12g (⅜oz) of dark brown sugarpaste. Roll out 12g (⅜oz) of the mixed paste to a 5mm (¼in) thickness and using a cutter, take out a 4cm (1½in) circle. Soften the remaining sugarpaste with white vegetable fat (shortening) before placing into the sugar press. Run a line of glue around the base of the nest and extrude the strands, layering them one group on top of the other until you have formed the nest (**D**).

THE EGGS

Take 6g (⅛oz) of white modelling paste and divide into three for the small eggs. Roll each into a round ball then shape into an oval (**D**) and place the eggs inside the nest.

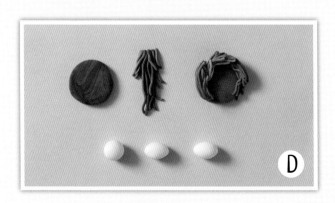

The Artist

This creative topper is a masterpiece in itself! An eccentric French artist has found his latest muse and is keen to get stuck into his paints to bring his vision to life. At this rate, however, there will be more paint on his clothes and the floor than on his easel!

You will need:

Sugarpaste
- 69g (2½oz) grey
- 53g (4oz) white
- 35g (1¼oz) black
- 29g (1⅛oz) flesh
- 23g (⅞oz) teddy bear brown
- 20g (¾oz) red
- 10g (¼oz) dark blue
- 1g (⅛oz) green
- 1g (⅛oz) blue
- 1g (⅛oz) orange
- 1g (⅛oz) yellow

Materials
- 60g (2¼oz) white modelling paste
- White vegetable fat (shortening)
- CMC (Tylose)
- White paste food colour or white edible paint
- Rainbow Dust edible silver paint
- Edible glue

Equipment
- 2cm (¾in) hexagonal cutter
- 2cm (¾in) and 10cm (4in) circle cutter
- Cocktail stick (toothpick)
- Basic tool kit (see Modelling Cake Toppers)

The paint tube

1. **For the paint tube** roll 60g (2¼oz) of white modelling paste into a fat sausage shape. Flatten with your hand, making the bottom of the tube slightly wider than the top. Thin out the bottom of the tube and curl it upwards (**A**). Flatten the centre of the paint tube to make it an irregular shape and to accommodate the artist's foot.

2. **To make the nozzle** add some CMC (Tylose) to 5g (⅛oz) of grey sugarpaste. Roll into a ball then pinch out the nozzle shape using your fingers. Make a straight cut at the back of the shape and mark around the base of the nozzle with tool no.4 (**A**). Push a short piece of dry spaghetti into the end of the tube and slip the nozzle over the top. Paint the nozzle with edible silver paint and a soft brush.

3. **Make the decorative stripes** using 6g (⅛oz) of red sugarpaste rolled out thinly. Cut one strip measuring 1 x 6cm (⅜ x 2½in) and another measuring 0.5 x 6cm (¼ x 2½in) (**A**). Attach across the top of the tube and trim off any excess.

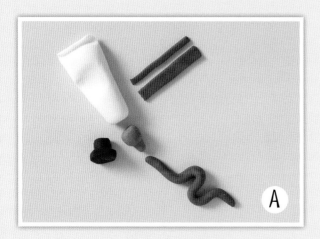

4. **To make the cap** you will need 5g (⅛oz) of black sugarpaste with CMC added. Roll out the sugarpaste to a 5mm (¼in) thickness and press a 2cm (¾in) hexagonal cutter into the paste to cut out the top. Roll the remainder of the paste into a fat sausage shape, trim to size and attach to the top of the cap (**A**).

TIP *If you do not have a hexagonal cutter for the paint tube cap, use a round one instead.*

5. **For the paint** you will need 8g (¼oz) of red sugarpaste rolled into an irregular sausage shape (**A**). Push a short piece of dry spaghetti into the end of the nozzle and attach the paint.

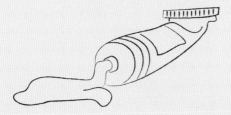

The paint palette and brush

THE PALETTE

1. **For the paint palette** you will need 2g (⅛oz) of teddy bear brown sugarpaste with CMC added, rolled into a fat cone shape. Flatten the shape with your finger then gently roll with a rolling pin to achieve the required shape. Take out the thumb hole with either a small round cutter or the end of tool no.11 (**B**).

2. **Make the paint splodges** by rolling oval shapes with tiny amounts taken from 1g (⅛oz) of each of the following sugarpaste colours: red, orange, blue, green and yellow. Attach around the palette then roll a small amount of flesh sugarpaste into a sausage shape to resemble a thumb and attach to the base (**B**). Set aside to dry.

THE PAINTBRUSH

1. **For the paintbrush handle** thinly roll out 2g (⅛oz) of dark blue sugarpaste and cut to measure 1 x 4cm (⅜ x 1½in) (**B**). From 1g (⅛oz) of grey sugarpaste, cut out a 1cm (⅜in) square and line this up at the end of the blue strip. Apply a line of glue down the centre of both pieces and place a length of dry spaghetti over the top, leaving 1cm (⅜in) showing at the end to take the bristles. Fold over the paste then trim off the excess with tool no.4, keeping the blade as close to the spaghetti as possible. Roll it over the worktop to thin it out even more and trim off the paste, keeping 1cm (⅜in) of the spaghetti showing at the top. Paint the metal end of the brush with edible silver paint.

B

2. **To make the bristles** take off a small amount from 1g (⅛oz) of teddy bear brown sugarpaste. Roll the paste into a cone shape and slip it over the end of the spaghetti at the top of the brush. Mark the bristles using tool no.4 then add some extra lines across the top of the blue sugarpaste and around the grey sugarpaste (**B**).

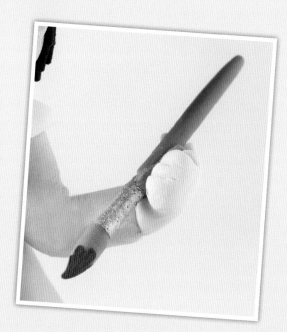

The artist

THE SHOES AND SOCKS

1. **To make the shoes** you will need 17g (⅝oz) of black sugarpaste with some CMC added. Equally divide then roll each piece into a fat cone shape (**C**).

2. **Make two sock tops** using 4g (⅛oz) of red sugarpaste with CMC added. Roll into a short sausage shape and cut into two. Attach to the top of each shoe and slip a short piece of dry spaghetti down through the centre, leaving 3cm (1¼in) showing at the top (**C**).

THE BODY AND LEGS

1. **For the body and legs** you will need to thoroughly knead half a teaspoon of CMC into 63g (2⅜oz) of grey sugarpaste. Roll into a carrot shape and flatten slightly with your hand. Divide for the legs at the wider end, putting the point of tool no.4 in the centre of the shape. Round off all the edges and lengthen the legs, shaping the trousers as you do so (**C**). The right leg is to be kept straight, while the left leg should be bent at the knee area, making it shorter. Push a short piece of dry spaghetti into each shoulder while the paste is soft.

2. Slip the shoes and socks into the ends of the trouser legs. Secure the left shoe to the top of the tube of paint and support the body at the back to keep it in place until dry.

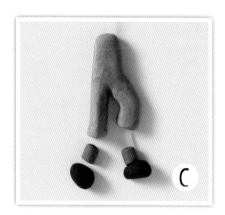

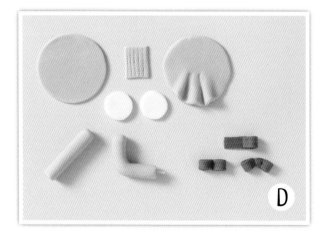

THE ARTIST'S SMOCK

1. **To complete the smock** you will need 40g (1½oz) of white sugarpaste mixed with 20g (¾oz) of teddy bear brown sugarpaste to create a light cream shade. Take off 40g (1½oz) of the mixed paste and roll out evenly. Use the larger cutter to cut out a 10cm (4in) circle and slip over the spaghetti at the artist's neck. Bring the folds forward, define into smaller folds using the end of your paintbrush then arrange around the rest of the body like a skirt (**D**).

2. **For the smocked front** take off a further 2g (⅛oz) of the mixed paste and thinly roll out to measure 2.5 x 2cm (1 x ¾in). Mark vertical lines using tool no.12 (**D**) and attach the piece to the front of the smock. Add some paint splashes on the front of the smock using tiny amounts of red and blue sugarpaste made into irregular shapes.

3. Roll the remainder of the mixed paste into a sausage shape for the arms measuring 14cm (5½in) in length. Divide equally and keeping the rounded end at the top of the arm, bend at the elbow (**D**). Insert a short piece of dry spaghetti into the wrist, leaving 1cm (⅜in) showing.

TIP *Leave the arms to harden off a little before proceeding with the hands.*

4. **To make the collar** roll out 12g (⅜oz) of white sugarpaste and take out two circles using a 2cm (¾in) round cutter. Secure on either side of the spaghetti at the neck (**D**).

5. **To make the floppy bow** roll out 1g (⅛oz) of red sugarpaste to measure 1 x 6cm (⅜ x 2½in). Apply some edible glue to the centre of the strip and turn each end to meet in the centre. You should now have two loops. Turn the piece over and pinch the edges underneath to narrow in the centre. Using tool no.4, mark two lines to create the centre and bend the bow downwards (**D**).

THE HANDS

1. **To make the hands** equally divide 3g (⅛oz) of flesh sugarpaste then roll each piece into a ball shape and then into a cone shape (**E**).

2. **To make the left hand** slightly flatten the cone shape and mark the thumb and index finger with tool no.4, rounding off any edges. The palm of the hand is facing upwards, so now curl over the rest of the hand and indent three fingers using tool no.4. Apply some edible glue to the palm and attach the paintbrush, bringing the fingers around the brush handle (**E**). Slip the hand over the spaghetti at the wrist and support until dry if necessary.

3. **To make the right hand** roll the remaining flesh sugarpaste into a cone shape then make a straight cut at the wrist. Apply some glue to the palm, attach the palette, slip over the spaghetti at the wrist and support until dry.

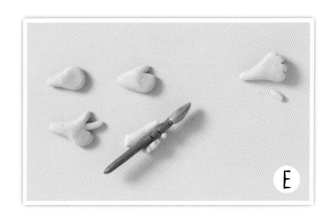

E

THE HEAD

1. **To make the head** you will need 23g (⅞oz) of flesh sugarpaste with a good pinch of CMC added. Roll into a smooth ball and from underneath the ball, pull down the neck in a twisting movement. Make a straight cut at the base of the neck. Place the ball into the palm of your hand and indent the eye area with your little finger, keeping the head softly rounded (**F**).

2. **To make the nose** take off enough from 2g (⅛oz) of flesh sugarpaste to make a small cone shape and attach to the centre of the face. Set the leftover paste aside. Using tool no.5, make two small holes for the nostrils (**F**).

3. **To make the mouth** use the large end of tool no.5 to mark a smile then flatten the top lip into a straight line with tool no.4. Roll a tiny banana shape from 1g (⅛oz) of white sugarpaste for the top teeth and insert the teeth into the mouth, underneath the straight top lip. Take off a tiny amount of the flesh sugarpaste and roll another banana shape to make the bottom lip (**F**).

4. **For the eyes** take off enough from the leftover white sugarpaste to make two small eyeballs and position them on the face. From 3g (⅛oz) of black sugarpaste add a tiny dot on top of each eyeball for the pupils. Add tiny tapered cone shapes for the eyelids and position them over the eyes. To make the eyebrows roll a thin lace of black sugarpaste into two arches and place over each eye (**F**). Set the leftover black sugarpaste aside.

5. Using the rounded end of tool no.4, mark two vertical lines between the eyes and add a few horizontal frown marks to the forehead. To highlight the eyes, dip the end of the cocktail stick into some white paste food colour or white edible paint and add a dot to each pupil.

F

TIP *Make sure the eyeballs are fairly small, as they will increase in size when you press them down.*

THE HAIR AND BERET

1. **To complete the hair** you will need 10g (¼oz) of black sugarpaste with white vegetable fat (shortening) added to soften it. Take off a small amount to create two tapered cone shapes for the side burns, attach to each side of the face and mark the hairs with tool no.4 (**F**).

2. Cover the head with a layer of edible glue, fill the cup of the sugar press with the softened black paste then extrude lengths of hair, taking it off in layers rather than clumps (**F**). Attach the hair to the head beginning at the back of the neck, bringing it up to the crown then working your way around to the sides.

3. **To shape the beret** roll 8g (¼oz) of dark blue sugarpaste into a ball and hollow it out with your fingers (**F**). Attach off-centre to one side of the head.

6. **To make the ears** use the leftover flesh sugarpaste and roll two equally sized small balls into cone shapes. Attach to the sides of the head, indenting the bottom of the ears with the end of your paintbrush (**F**).

7. **For the moustache** take off a small amount of black sugarpaste and roll two very small balls. Form them into tapered cone shapes, turn up at the ends and place directly underneath the nose. Roll the same amount for the beard into a flattened cone shape, attach under the bottom lip and mark lines for the hair with tool no.4 (**F**).

Mucky Pup

Somebody is in deep trouble when his owner returns! This mischievous pooch is finding the paint such a wonderful plaything and making a fine mess of the polished wooden floors – surely it was just an innocent accident?

You will need:

Sugarpaste

- 150g (5½oz) teddy bear brown
- 84g (3oz) grey
- 21g (¾oz) pale blue
- 4g (⅛oz) black
- 1g (⅛oz) pink

Materials

- 98g (3½oz) white modelling paste
- White vegetable fat (shortening)
- Sugarflair dark brown paste food colour
- Rainbow dust edible paint in pearlescent light silver and pale blue
- Edible glue

Equipment

- FMM wood impression mat
- 2cm (¾in) circle cutter
- Basic tool kit (see Modelling Cake Toppers)

The dog

THE BODY AND LEGS

1. **To make the body** roll 53g (1⅞oz) of grey sugarpaste with CMC (Tylose) added into a fat cone shape. Place the shape onto a card in a lying position then lift up the back end of the cone and support with foam (**A**).

2. Apply a coat of edible glue over the body. Soften 30g (1⅛oz) of grey sugarpaste with white vegetable fat (shortening) and fill the cup of the sugar press (or garlic press). Extrude short strands to make the hair then use to cover the body (**A**).

3. **For the front paws** you will need 14g (½oz) of white modelling paste equally divided. Roll each piece into a fat cone shape and make a diagonal cut at the top. Using the rounded end of tool no.4, mark the paws using long vertical strokes to resemble hair. Push a piece of dry spaghetti into the end of each leg and insert into each side of the body (**A**).

4. **For the back paws** make only the white paws using 8g (¼oz) of white modelling paste, equally divided and rolled into two fat cone shapes. Using the rounded end of tool no.4, mark the paws as in Step 3 (**A**) and attach to either side of the body.

THE HEAD

1. **To make the head** roll 30g (1⅛oz) of white modelling paste into a smooth ball and indent half of the ball to shape the muzzle (**A**). Using tool no.4, mark a line down the front of the face. At the top of the line, mark a hole for the nose with the pointed end of tool no.3, then at the bottom of the line, mark a smile with tool no.11. Use the pointed end of tool no.3 to make a hole to open the mouth in the centre of the smile and to indent two holes for the eyes. Using the rounded end of tool no.4, feather all around the sides and back of the head.

TIP *Make sure the dog's head is square rather than long.*

2. **To make the tongue** you will need 1g (⅛oz) of pink sugarpaste rolled into a sausage shape (**A**). Push one end into the mouth and indent a line down the centre with tool no.4.

3. **For the eyes** take off enough from 1g (⅛oz) of black sugarpaste to make two small balls and attach into the holes (**A**). Set the rest aside.

4. **Begin to build up the face** by taking 1g (⅛oz) of white modelling paste and rolling into a flattened cone shape. Mark lines down the shape with tool no.4 then make a straight cut at the top. Place this at the centre of the muzzle and bring it down around the cheeks. Make another piece in the same way using 1g (⅛oz) of white modelling paste for the other side (**A**).

5. **To make the nose** take off enough from the leftover black sugarpaste to make a small cone shape (**A**) and attach inside the hole at the end of the muzzle.

6. **Add two eyebrows** by dividing 1g (⅛oz) of white modelling paste equally and rolling each piece into a

flattened cone shape. Mark the lines with tool no.4 then arch the pieces and attach around each eye (**A**).

7. **To make the ears** equally divide 2g (⅛oz) of white modelling paste and make two flattened cone shapes. Using the rounded end of tool no.4, feather the lines on the ears (**A**) and attach to each side of the head.

8. **Make a fringe** using a further 1g (⅛oz) of white modelling paste rolled into a flattened cone shape and feathered with the rounded end of tool no.4. Arrange the fringe from the back of the head and over one eye (**A**). Using a soft paintbrush, add some touches of pearlescent light silver paint to one ear and the fringe.

The wooden floorboards

1. **To complete the wooden floorboards** you will need 150g (5½oz) of teddy bear brown sugarpaste with CMC added. Roll out with a rolling pin then place an FMM wood impression mat over the top and roll over again to make the woodgrain impression.

2. Trim around the edges to make the paste the size of the mat and divide the piece into two planks. Make two and set them out in an irregular shape (**B**). Secure the completed dog to the wooden floor with edible glue.

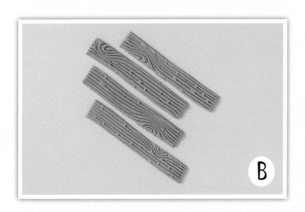

B

TIP *If you do not have an impression mat or textured rolling pin you can mark the lines on the planks with the rounded end of tool no. 4.*

The paint can and brush

THE PAINT CAN

1. **To make the paint can** you will need 20g (¾oz) of white modelling paste, rolled into a fat sausage shape and flattened at both ends with your finger (**C**). Mark a circle at the top of the pot with a 2cm (¾in) circle cutter and place the paint can on its side beside the dog. Make a band to go around the paint can using 3g (⅛oz) of black sugarpaste, rolled out and cut into a strip measuring 1 x 7cm (⅜ x 2¾in).

2. **To create the spilled paint** take 10g (¼oz) of pale blue sugarpaste, flatten between your fingers and pull out the edges to resemble moving paint. Attach the first piece a little away from the can. Take a further 10g (¼oz) of the blue sugarpaste and shape again, this time attaching one end to the can and overlapping the first paint spill (**C**). Add some further spots of paint here and there. Using a soft brush, paint on some pearlescent pale blue edible paint.

THE PAINTBRUSH

1. **To make the paintbrush** take 20g (¾oz) of white modelling paste and colour with some dark brown paste food colour. Roll the paste into a ball then lengthen the ball with your finger, pulling out the handle. Press the other end with your finger, making a wooden spoon shape. Using tool no.4, make a straight cut halfway across the rounded end (**C**).

2. **To make the bristles** roll 1g (⅛oz) of grey sugarpaste into a flattened sausage shape. Using tool no.4, mark the bristles and attach to the end of the paintbrush (**C**).

3. Roll 1g (⅛oz) of blue sugarpaste into a sausage shape and flatten. Attach to the end of the bristles then paint on some pale blue pearlescent edible paint (**C**).

4. Attach the paintbrush to the floor and place the dog's paw over the handle. Add a little of the pale blue pearlescent paint to the dog's paws.

Daisy's Birthday

Daisy the cow is in the mood for a celebration, sitting expectantly in her finest floral headband beside her party cracker and birthday cake, complete with a pretty pink candle. Now all she needs are her friends to arrive to really get the party started!

You will need:

Sugarpaste

- 8g (¼oz) teddy bear brown
- 7g (¼oz) pink
- 5g (⅛oz) red
- 3g (⅛oz) black

Materials

- 212g (7½oz) white modelling paste
- White vegetable fat (shortening)
- Rainbow Dust pearlescent cerise edible paint
- Rainbow Dust pink edible heart sprinkles
- Edible glue

Equipment

- 3cm (1¼in), 2cm (¾in) circle cutters
- 6mm (¼in), 1cm (⅜in), 13mm (½in) blossom cutters
- 7.5cm (3in) cake card
- Textured rolling pin (optional)
- Basic tool kit (see Modelling Cake Toppers)

Daisy the cow

THE BODY

1. **To complete the cow** you will need 127g (4½oz) of white modelling paste. Take off 43g (1⅝oz) and roll into a cone shape for the body (**A**). Keeping the shape upright, push a piece of dry spaghetti down through the centre, leaving 2cm (¾in) showing at the top.

2. **Make the back legs** using 24g (1oz) of white modelling paste rolled into a smooth sausage shape. Using tool no.4, make a diagonal cut in the centre and press the other ends flat with your finger. Apply edible glue to the diagonal cuts and attach the legs to the sides of the body, gently curving them to shape them (**A**). Push a short piece of dry spaghetti into the end of each leg.

3. **Make the front legs** in the same way using a further 24g (1oz) of white modelling paste, this time

positioning the diagonal cut on the shoulder at the top of the cone (**A**). Position the arms so that the left arm is resting on the leg and the right arm is at the side of the cow. Push a short piece of dry spaghetti into the ends as before.

4. **Make the tail** using 3g (⅛oz) of the remaining sugarpaste rolled into a tapered cone shape. Using the rounded end of tool no.4, mark downward lines at the end of the tail (**A**) and attach to the back of the cow.

5. **To complete four hooves** you will need 12g (⅜oz) of flesh sugarpaste divided equally into four. Roll each piece into a ball then into a fat cone shape. Attach a hoof to the end of each leg, pushing them on firmly with the flat part of your finger and turning them outwards to give movement. Using the rounded end of tool no.4, mark a line in the centre of each hoof (**A**).

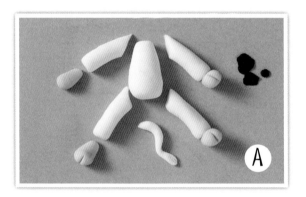

THE HEAD

1. **To make the head** roll 43g (1⅝oz) of white modelling paste into a ball by rolling it on the work surface using your little finger, then indent half of the ball to form the head shape (**B**). Shorten the face by slicing off the front with tool no.4. Push two short pieces of dry spaghetti into the front of the head and two more into the sides to support the ears.

2. **To make the nose** take 3g (⅛oz) of flesh sugarpaste and roll into a fat sausage shape. Flatten the shape with your finger and narrow in the centre (**B**). Attach to the front of the face, making good contact. Push the end of a paintbrush into the top corners to form the nostrils, lifting upwards as you do so. Slip the head over the spaghetti at the top of the body and secure with edible glue.

3. **To make the tongue** mix 1g (⅛oz) of red sugarpaste with 1g (⅛oz) of white modelling paste to create a deep pink shade. Take off a small amount for the tongue and roll into a flattened cone shape. Attach under the nose in the centre and set the leftover paste aside. From 1g (⅛oz) of white modelling paste, take off a small amount to make the bottom lip (**B**), roll into a flattened cone shape and attach underneath the tongue.

4. **For the eyes** roll two small balls of white modelling paste and position them fairly close together. Take off a tiny amount from 3g (⅛oz) of black sugarpaste and roll into two small balls for the pupils then press them onto the white eyeballs. Roll a very thin tapered loop and apply over each eye to outline (**B**). Set the leftover black sugarpaste aside.

5. **To make the ears** equally divide the remaining 3g (⅛oz) of white modelling paste and shape each piece into a flattened cone shape. Add a pink inner to each ear using 2g (⅛oz) of pink sugarpaste equally divided, with each piece rolled again into a flattened cone shape. Attach to the centre of each ear, slightly flattening with your finger (**B**). Make straight cuts at the narrow ends with tool no.4 and slip the ears over the spaghetti at the sides of the head.

6. **Make the black markings** using the leftover black sugarpaste, taking off small amounts and flattening between your finger and thumb to make irregular shapes (**A**). Add to the top of Daisy's ears and around her body.

TIP *Be careful not to make the nose too big and heavy and tilt the completed head to one side to give it attitude.*

THE HEADBAND AND FLOWERS

1. **For the headband** roll out the remaining mixed deep pink sugarpaste and cut out a strip measuring 0.3 x 4cm (⅛ x 1½in) (**B**). Bend in a curved shape, apply edible glue and place across the head between the ears.

2. **To make the flowers** roll out 2g (⅛oz) of yellow sugarpaste and cut out two flower shapes using the 1cm (⅜in) blossom cutter. Using the 6mm (¼in) blossom cutter, take out a further shape from yellow sugarpaste (**B**).

3. From 1g (⅛oz) of white modelling paste, use the blossom cutters to cut out one 1cm (⅜in) and one 6mm (¼in) flower shape. Attach the large white shape over the larger yellow shape and add a dot of yellow sugarpaste to the centre to form a flower. Add a dot of white modelling paste in the centre of the smaller yellow flower (**B**). Attach the flowers to each side of the headband.

The birthday cake and candle

THE BIRTHDAY CAKE

1. **To make the cake** mix 10g (¼oz) of white modelling paste with 8g (¼oz) of teddy bear brown sugarpaste. Roll out the mixed paste to a thickness of 1cm (⅜in) and use the cutter to take out two 3cm (1⅛in) circles: one for the top and one for the bottom of the cake (**C**).

2. Place the bottom layer on a cake card then take 4g (⅛oz) of white modelling paste and soften with white vegetable fat (shortening). Roll into a ball and flatten, pulling out the sides to look like dripping cream, and attach over the top of the base. Roll out 5g (⅛oz) of red sugarpaste to make a jam layer, cut out a 3cm (1¼in) circle then place

over the cream layer. Finally add the top layer. Push a short piece of spaghetti into the centre of the cake, leaving 1cm (⅜in) showing at the top. Decorate the top of the cake with pink edible heart sprinkles (**C**).

THE ROSE CANDLEHOLDER

1. **To make the candleholder** roll out 5g (⅛oz) of pink sugarpaste into a thin sausage shape and roll with the edge of a rolling pin to thin out. Take one end of the sugarpaste and curl it inwards then open the edges with your finger to form the rose shape (**C**).

2. Make a straight cut at the end and slip the rose over the spaghetti in the centre of the cake. Using the end of your paintbrush, make a hole in the centre of the rose to allow the candle to be inserted. Paint the edges of the rose petals with pearlescent cerise edible paint.

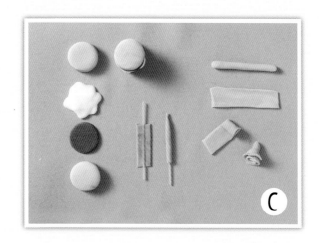

THE CANDLE

1. **To make the candle** add a little pink sugarpaste to 5g (⅛oz) of white modelling paste, roll out thinly and cut out a shape measuring 1 x 4cm (⅜ x 2¾in) (**C**). Run a line of edible glue down the centre and place a length of dry spaghetti on the top. Fold over the paste and cut off any excess as close to the spaghetti as possible.

2. Roll the candle on the work surface to shape, pinching out the top to form the wick. Leave some spaghetti showing at the base of the candle (**C**) then insert it into the centre of the rose.

The party cracker

1. **To make the cracker** you will need 22g (¾oz) of white modelling paste. Take off 5g (⅛oz) and roll into a sausage shape measuring 3.5cm (1⅜in) in length (**D**). Push a short piece of dry spaghetti through the centre, leaving a small amount showing at each end.

2. **Make a textured covering** by rolling out 5g (⅛oz) of white modelling paste and running a textured rolling pin over the surface (**D**). Cut a 4 x 3cm (1½ x 1¼in) strip and glue around the sausage shape.

3. **Make the frilled ends** of the cracker using 12g (⅜oz) of white modelling paste rolled out and cut into six 2cm (¾in) circles using a cutter. Frill around the edges to thin them out by placing the end of your paintbrush on the edge of the circle and gently rolling the brush into the paste using your index finger (**D**). Attach the frills together one on top of the other and secure over the spaghetti at the end of the cracker.

TIP *If you do not have a textured rolling pin you can roll small dots and add them instead of stars.*

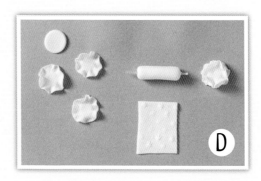

First-class Meerkat

This highly intelligent meerkat is looking very chuffed on his Graduation day. Clutching his prized degree scroll and proudly donning his smart gown and mortarboard, he grins with glee as he sits upon a stack of books for all to behold.

You will need:

Sugarpaste

- 61g (2¼oz) red
- 57g (2⅛oz) light brown
- 44g (1⅝oz) green
- 28g (1⅛oz) dark brown
- 18g (¾oz) black
- 6g (⅛oz) yellow
- 1g (⅛oz) white

Materials

- 144g (5¼oz) white modelling paste
- CMC (Tylose)
- Rainbow Dust dark brown edible dust
- Edible glue

Equipment

- 6cm (2⅜in), 5cm (2in), 4cm (1¾in), 3cm (1¼in) square cutters
- Florist wire no. 26 gauge, one length
- Soft brush
- Basic tool kit (see Modelling Cake Toppers)

The stack of books

THE RED BOOK

1. **To make the pages** for the red book, you will need 75g (2¾oz) of white modelling paste rolled out thinly. Cut out eight pages using a 6cm (2⅜in) square cutter and place them neatly one on top of the other (**A**).

TIP *Using modelling paste will allow you to make very thin pages. Make these first so the cover does not dry out and crack when folded over.*

2. **To make the cover** roll out 60g (2¼oz) of red sugarpaste with CMC (Tylose) added. Cut out a rectangle measuring 7 x 14cm (2¾ x 5½in) (**A**).

3. Place the pages on one side of the cover and bring the opposite side over the top of them (**A**). Take the 6cm (2⅜in) square cutter and gently indent a square shape on the book cover then set aside to dry.

THE GREEN BOOK

To make the green book you will need 35g (1¼oz) of white modelling paste for the pages. Roll out thinly and cut out seven pages using a 5cm (2in) square cutter. For the cover you will need 44g (1⅝oz) of green sugarpaste with CMC added, rolled out and cut to a measurement of 6 x 12cm (2⅜ x 4½in) (**A**). Assemble as described for the red book.

THE BROWN BOOK

1. **To make the brown book** you will need 30g (1⅛oz) of white modelling paste for the pages. Roll out thinly and cut out seven pages using a 4cm (1½in) square cutter. For the cover you will need 28g (1⅛oz) of dark brown sugarpaste with CMC added, rolled out and cut to a measurement of 6 x 12cm (2⅜ x 4½in) (**A**). Assemble as described for the red book.

2. Stack the books on top of each other at an angle, with the red book at the bottom, the green book in the centre and the brown book on the top.

A

The meerkat

THE BODY

1. **For the body** you will need 24g (1oz) of light brown sugarpaste rolled into a tall cone shape (**B**). Place the cone in an upright position on top of the brown book and push a length of dry spaghetti down through the centre.

2. **To make the back legs** equally divide 12g (⅜oz) of light brown sugarpaste and roll each piece into a sausage shape. Thin half of each leg by rolling on the work surface and turning up the ends for the feet (**B**). Attach the legs to the meerkat's hipline, bending slightly at the knees.

3. **To make the chest hair** mix 1g (⅛oz) of light brown sugarpaste with 1g (⅛oz) of white sugarpaste to make a lighter shade. Shape into a long cone and flatten with your finger. Use the rounded end of tool no.4 to feather the piece, making a line down the centre to finish (**B**). Attach to the front of the meerkat, blending the edges of the hair into the body.

4. **For the arms** roll 6g (⅛oz) of light brown sugarpaste into a sausage shape, thin at the top and make a diagonal cut in the centre (**B**). Attach to the body, bringing them around to the front ready for the scroll to be attached in position later.

5. **To make the tail** roll 3g (⅛oz) of light brown sugarpaste into a long tapered cone shape and attach to the back of meerkat (**B**).

THE HEAD

1. **To make the head** you will need to roll 10g (¼oz) of light brown sugarpaste into a short cone shape. Indent the eyes with the pointed end of tool no.3 (**B**).

2. **Form two small eyeballs** from 1g (⅛oz) of white modelling paste and secure them inside the sockets. Take off and roll two very small balls from 1g (⅛oz) of black sugarpaste for the pupils (**B**) and attach to the eyeballs by gently pressing them on with your finger.

3. **For the nose** take off enough of the black sugarpaste to make a small ball and attach at the end of the snout. Make two more small flattened balls for the ears (**B**).

4. **Make two eyebrows** from 1g (⅛oz) of light brown sugarpaste, taking off a small amount to make a tapered cone shape (**B**). Add one over each eye and with the rounded end of tool no.4, mark lines using light upward strokes. Place the head over the spaghetti at the neck. Use a soft brush to dust around the eyes and nose with dark brown edible dust.

THE SPECTACLES

1. **To make the spectacles**, take off two 5cm (2in) pieces from one length of no. 26 florist wire. Twist the two pieces together tightly three times in the centre to make the bridge (**C**).

2. Insert the handle of a paintbrush between the wires and proceed to twist them together tightly to form a lens (**C**). Remove the brush and repeat on the other side. Trim the length of wire and place the finished spectacles onto the meerkat's head.

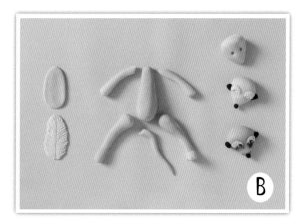

THE COLLAR

To make the collar roll out 6g (⅛oz) of black sugarpaste and 6g (⅛oz) of yellow sugarpaste. Cut each into a strip measuring 3 x 6cm (1¼ x 2⅜in) and curve out the lower edges to reduce the thickness in the centre. Attach around the shoulders, with the black collar over the yellow, draping over the back of the meerkat (**C**).

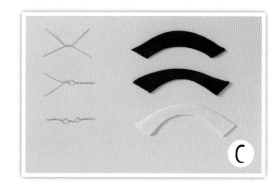

The scroll and mortarboard

THE SCROLL

1. **To make the scroll** thinly roll out 3g (⅛oz) of white modelling paste, cut out a 4cm (1½in) square and roll up into the scroll shape (**D**).

2. **To make the ribbon** take 1g (⅛oz) of red sugarpaste and cut out a narrow strip measuring 4cm (1½in) in length. Wrap around the scroll and cut out a small square to place on the top (**D**). Allow the scroll to dry and position on the meerkat's knees with the paws secured around it.

THE MORTARBOARD

1. **To complete the cap** you will need 11g (¼oz) of black sugarpaste. Take off 6g (⅛oz) and roll into a ball for the cap then hollow out the inside with your fingers to fit the head (**D**). Make a point at the centre front and secure to the top of the head.

2. **To make the mortarboard** roll out the remaining black sugarpaste, cut out a 3cm (1¼in) square (**D**) and attach to the top of the cap.

3. **Make the tassel** by taking off enough from the remaining black sugarpaste to roll into a short sausage shape and marking a line around the top using tool no.4. Using the rounded end of tool no.4, mark lines with downward strokes to form the tassels then attach to the top of the mortarboard (**D**).

TIP *Make the top of the mortarboard a little in advance to ensure that it stays in shape.*

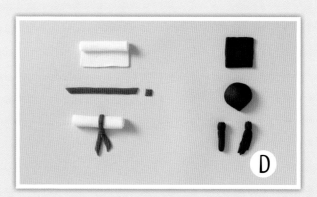

Summertime Suzie

Suzie is such a laid-back duck and loves nothing better than to relax in her rubber ring in the cool sea on a hot summer's day. When she tires of playing with her beach ball she can retreat from the sun into her quaint little beach hut for a well-deserved snooze. What summertime bliss!

You will need:

Sugarpaste

- 56g (2oz) pale blue
- 35g (1¼oz) yellow
- 35g (1¼oz) white
- 29g (1⅛oz) red
- 25g (1oz) light brown
- 15g (½oz) dark blue
- 7g (¼oz) lime green
- 3g (⅛oz) black
- 2g (⅛oz) dark green

Materials

- 236g (8¼oz) white modelling paste
- CMC (Tylose)
- White vegetable fat (shortening)
- Edible glue

Equipment

- 10cm (4in) cake card
- 3cm (1¼in) circle cutter
- 6mm (¼in), 1cm (⅜in), 12mm (½in), 15mm (⅝in) square cutters
- Basic tool kit (see Modelling Cake Toppers)

Suzie the duck

THE RUBBER RING AND WATER

1. **To complete the rubber ring** roll 110g (3⅞oz) of white modelling paste into a sausage shape measuring 23cm (9in) in length. Make a neat join at the back of the ring (**A**) and place onto a 10cm (4in) cake card.

2. **For the red stripes** roll out 8g (¼oz) of red sugarpaste and cut out a strip measuring 1.5 x 18cm (⅝ x 7in). Cut into four pieces, attach the first piece over the join at the back of the ring and space the other three out evenly (**A**).

3. **To make the water** mix 25g (1oz) of white sugarpaste randomly with 5g (⅛oz) of dark blue sugarpaste. Add drops of water then mix with a pallet knife to make a very soft paste. Apply the paste around the edge of the board and to the sides of the ring (**A**).

SUZIE'S BODY

1. **To make the body** roll 50g (1¾oz) of white modelling paste into a cone shape measuring 7cm (2¾in) in height (**B**). Place inside the swimming ring and push a piece of dry spaghetti down through the centre, leaving 2cm (¾in) showing at the top.

2. **Make the legs** using 12g (⅜oz) of yellow sugarpaste with CMC (Tylose) added. Divide the paste equally and roll each piece into a sausage shape. Keep one end of each leg a little thicker and turn these ends upwards to form the feet. Widen the feet with your finger and mark the edges with the rounded end of tool no.4 (**B**). Push short pieces of dry spaghetti into the hipline of the body and slip the legs over so that they rest on the rubber ring.

3. **For the wings** equally divide 14g (½oz) of white modelling paste and roll each piece into a wooden spoon shape. Flatten the ends slightly with your finger, mark the tips with tool no.4 then indent the rest of each wing with two lines (**B**). Push short pieces of dry spaghetti into the shoulder line of the body and slip the wings over. Attach the tip of the right wing to the side of the head and position the left ring so that it rests on the rubber ring.

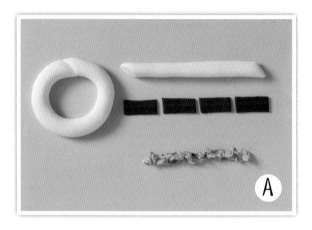

TIP *For best results, the mixed sugarpaste for the water should be soft enough so that it stands up in peaks.*

SUZIE'S HEAD

1. **To make the head** roll 20g (¾oz) of white modelling paste into a smooth ball then into a fat cone shape (**C**). Push a short piece of dry spaghetti into the centre of the head to hold the beak.

2. **For the beak** you will need 3g (⅛oz) of yellow sugarpaste rolled into a small tapered cone shape. Shape and flatten out the upper part then fold it over the pointed end to form the beak shape (**C**) and attach to the spaghetti on the head.

3. **Make the tongue** by taking off a tiny amount from 1g (⅛oz) of orange sugarpaste to make a cone shape and flattening with your finger (**C**). Apply some edible glue to the inside of the beak and place the tongue inside.

4. **To make the eyes** take off enough from 4g (⅛oz) of white modelling paste to make two small oval shapes and place them just above the beak (**C**). Set the remaining modelling paste aside. From 1g (⅛oz) of black sugarpaste, take off enough to make two tiny pupils and place on top of the white eyeballs, pressing lightly with your finger. Roll two very thin laces from black sugarpaste to outline the tops of the eyes (**C**).

5. **For the cheeks** equally divide 2g (⅛oz) of white modelling paste, make two banana shapes (**C**) and secure on either side of the beak. Using some of the remaining white modelling paste, make two banana shapes for the eyebrows and attach over the eyes. Make three tapered cone shapes for the hair and attach to the top of the head.

THE BIKINI

1. **To complete the bikini** you will need 7g (¼oz) of lime green sugarpaste and 1g (⅛oz) of dark green sugarpaste. To make the bikini bottoms, roll out 6g (⅛oz) of lime green sugarpaste to measure 2 x 6cm (¾ x 1⅜in). Using a 3cm (1¼in) circle cutter, take out the legs to shape the bikini bottoms (**D**). Attach to the duck and adjust if necessary at this point.

2. **For the bikini top** roll out the remaining lime green paste and cut out a 1.5cm (⅝in) square. Equally divide the square to make two triangular shapes and secure them to the duck's chest. Use 1g (⅛oz) of dark green sugarpaste to outline the top and bottom of the bikini and add the spots (**D**).

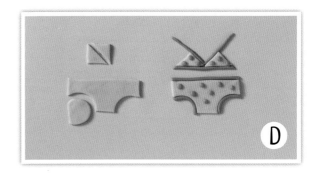

The beach ball

1. **To make the beach ball** roll 50g (1¾oz) of white modelling paste into a smooth ball. To make the covering you will need 10g (¼oz) each of dark blue, pale blue, white and yellow sugarpaste. Soften each of the colours with white vegetable fat (shortening) and divide into small balls (**E**).

2. Marble the colours by pushing them together and rolling them into a soft ball then roll out into a 10cm (4in) circle (**E**). Apply some edible glue around the white ball and wrap the covering around it. Trim off any excess and continue to smooth out the ball.

The beach hut

1. **For the hut** take 46g (1⅝oz) of pale blue sugarpaste and add a good pinch of CMC. Roll the sugarpaste out to a 1cm (⅜in) thickness and cut out a rectangle measuring 5 x 6cm (2 x 2¼in). Mark the centre of the shape at the top, and then mark a line across to indicate the roof space. Make a diagonal cut from the centre point to that line to angle the shape of the roof on both sides. Mark further horizontal lines across the front of the hut to look like planks of wood (**F**). Push two pieces of dry spaghetti through the bottom of the hut, leaving 1cm (⅜in) showing. Set the leftover pale blue sugarpaste aside.

TIP *Allow time for the hut to dry before standing it upright.*

2. **To make the roof** roll 14g (½oz) of red sugarpaste into a strip measuring 1.5 x 8cm (⅝ x 3¼in). Attach to the top of the hut, marking lines across with tool no.4 (**F**).

3. **To make the red door** take 7g (¼oz) of red sugarpaste and cut out a piece measuring 3 x 2cm (1¼ x ¾in). Use tool no.4 to mark vertical lines down the door (**F**). Attach to the left side of the hut then roll a tiny ball from blue sugarpaste for the doorknob and add in place.

4. **For the windows** you will need 2g (⅛oz) of black sugarpaste rolled out thinly. Using a 1cm (⅜in) cutter, take out one square and attach to the top centre of the hut. To make the window frame roll out 2g (⅛oz) of the pale blue sugarpaste and use the cutter to take out a 1cm (⅜in) square. Using a 6mm (¼in) square cutter, take out the centre of the square and attach over the windowpane (**F**).

5. Use a 12mm (½in) square cutter to take out another square from the black sugarpaste and position opposite the door. Roll two tiny strips of the leftover blue paste and crisscross them to make the windowpanes. Make the window frame for this window by cutting out a 12mm (½in) square from the blue sugarpaste and then using a 1cm (⅜in) cutter to take out the centre of the square. Attach this over the windowpane (**F**).

6. **To make the house support** you will need 25g (1oz) of light brown sugarpaste with CMC added. Roll the paste into a sausage shape measuring 6cm (2⅜in) long. Press tool no.5 down the centre of the sausage to indent it, making a ridge deep enough to support the house (**F**). Apply some edible glue to the piece and push the house into the centre. Secure the sides to the front and back of the house for more support.

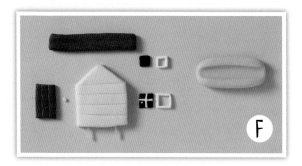

Halloween Frog

This spooky amphibian is all dressed up and ready to go trick or treating on Halloween night, accompanied by a little ladybird hitching a lift on his pumpkin. With his pointed witch's hat and scary stare, he is sure to give you a fright when he knocks on your door!

You will need:

Sugarpaste

- 132g (4¾oz) green
- 37g (1¼oz) orange
- 11g (¼oz) purple
- 2g (⅛oz) white
- 1g (⅛oz) black
- 1g (⅛oz) yellow
- 1g (⅛oz) red
- 1g (⅛oz) dark brown
- 1g (⅛oz) light brown

Materials

- White paste food colour
- CMC (Tylose)
- Edible glue

Equipment

- 4cm (1½in) circle cutter
- 8mm (⅜in), 13mm (½in) square cutters
- Cocktail stick (toothpick)
- Basic tool kit (see Modelling Cake Toppers)

The frog

THE BODY AND LEGS

1. **To create the frog** you will need 132g (4¾oz) of green sugarpaste with CMC (Tylose) added. Take off 58g (2¼oz) and roll into a tall cone shape for the body (**A**).

2. **For the back legs** you will need 30g (1⅛oz) of green sugarpaste equally divided. Roll each piece into a tapered cone shape measuring 10cm (4in) in length, keeping one end quite fat while narrowing the rest of the leg (**A**). Use tool no.4 to take out three 'V' shapes for the toes, round them off with your fingers, then use the rounded end of tool no.4 to mark lines down the centre of each toe. Attach the legs to the body and fold them over to the front.

3. **For the toenails** take off enough from 1g (⅛oz) of orange sugarpaste to roll out small balls (**A**) and attach to the end of each toe. Set the remaining paste aside.

THE HEAD

1. **To make the head** roll 28g (1⅛oz) of the green sugarpaste into a ball then into a wide cone shape (**A**). Using the edge of a 4cm (1¾in) circle cutter, mark a wide smile. Attach the head to the body and push a piece of dry spaghetti into the top of the head to take the hat.

> **TIP** *Insert the soft end of your paintbrush inside the mouth to soften it and open it up slightly in the centre.*

2. **Make the eyes** by equally dividing 2g (⅛oz) of the green sugarpaste and rolling each piece into a ball. Attach to the top of the head and indent the eye sockets using the pointed end of tool no.3. From 1g (⅛oz) of white sugarpaste, take off enough to make two small balls for the eyes (**A**) and insert into the sockets.

3. From 1g (⅛oz) of light brown sugarpaste, take off two much smaller balls for the irises and press them on top of the eyeballs. Make a pupil for each eye by taking off a tiny amount of black sugarpaste, rolling into a ball and pressing onto the top (**A**). Highlight the eyes by applying a small dot of white paste food colour with a cocktail stick (toothpick).

4. **To make the tongue** roll a tiny ball from 1g (⅛oz) of orange sugarpaste, flatten it (**A**) and insert into the centre of the mouth opening.

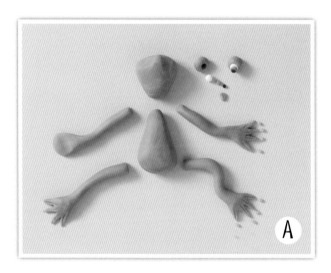

THE ARMS

1. **For the arms** equally divide the remaining 14g (½oz) of green sugarpaste. Roll out each arm to a length of 7cm (2¾in) and create as described for the back legs (**A**). Push a piece of dry spaghetti into each side of the body and attach the arms by slipping them over the top. The right arm should be attached to the pumpkin and the left arm to the side of the frog's head.

2. **For the toenails** roll tiny balls from 1g (⅛oz) of orange sugarpaste and attach to the ends of each toe (**A**).

The witch's hat

THE HAT

To complete the hat you will need 11g (¼oz) of purple sugarpaste. Roll the sugarpaste out, use a cutter to cut out a 4cm (1½in) circle and place over the spaghetti at the top of the head, shaping it over the contours of the frog's head to add movement. Roll the remaining paste into a cone shape and taper as shown (**B**). Secure to the centre of the hat brim.

THE BAND AND BUCKLE

1. **Make the band** using 2g (⅛oz) of orange sugarpaste rolled out thinly. Cut a strip measuring 1 x 6cm (⅜ x 2⅜in) and attach around the hat, joining it neatly at the back (**B**).

2. **For the buckle** roll out 1g (⅛oz) of yellow sugarpaste. Use cutters to cut out a 13mm (½in) square then form the frame by cutting out and removing an 8mm (⅜in) square from the centre. Attach to the centre of the orange band then using the leftover paste, roll a tiny oval shape for the prong and attach in the centre of the buckle (**B**).

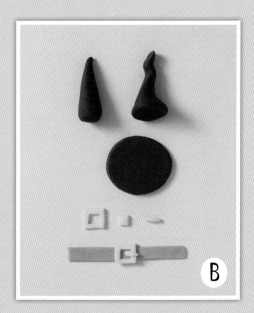

The pumpkin and ladybird

THE PUMPKIN

1. **To make the pumpkin** take 32g (1⅛oz) of orange sugarpaste, add some CMC and roll into a ball. Indent the top using the pointed end of tool no.3 and mark the sections around the side of the pumpkin with tool no.4 (**C**).

> **TIP** *Always use the rounded end of tool no.4 when indenting on round shapes, such as the pumpkin.*

2. **Make the stalk** by rolling 1g (⅛oz) of dark brown sugarpaste into a sausage shape. Cut to measure 2.5cm (1in) in length, make a diagonal cut at the top and shape the other end into a point (**C**). Insert into the hole at the top of the pumpkin.

3. **Make two very thin tendrils** using the paste cut off from the stalk. Curl the laces around the handle of your paintbrush to shape them, then slip them off and attach to the top of the pumpkin (**C**). Place the pumpkin at the front of the frog and attach the right arm to rest on top.

THE LADYBIRD

1. **To make the legs** take off enough from 1g (⅛oz) of black sugarpaste to roll into two very thin laces (**C**). Place them over the top of the pumpkin stalk.

> **TIP** *When modelling the tiny legs, condition your fingers with vegetable fat (shortening) to prevent them from sticking to the paste.*

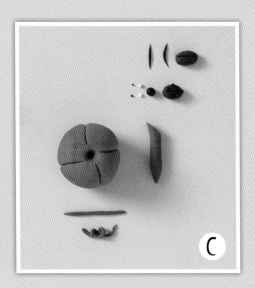

2. **For the body** take off enough from 1g (⅛oz) of red sugarpaste to make a small oval shape. Make a line down the centre top with tool no.4 and add some tiny black sugarpaste spots to the body (**C**).

3. **For the head** roll a small ball from black sugarpaste and attach to the front of the body. Make two tiny eyeballs from 1g (⅛oz) of white sugarpaste, attach to the head and finish with two smaller black sugarpaste balls for the pupils (**C**).

The Big Top

Roll up... roll up... all the fun of the circus coming is coming to town! The elephant and seal are eager to show off their tricks to an awestruck audience and there is plenty of room in the big top for all. Prepare to be entertained!

You will need:

Sugarpaste

- 89g (3oz) grey
- 61g (2¼oz) red
- 23g (⅞oz) blue
- 7g (¼oz) yellow
- 4g (⅛oz) fuchsia pink
- 4g (⅛oz) green
- 2g (⅛oz) black

Materials

- 304g (10½oz) white modelling paste
- CMC (Tylose)
- White edible paint
- Edible glue

Equipment

- 4cm (1½in) circle cutter
- 12mm (½in) square cutter
- Cocktail stick (toothpick)
- Basic tool kit (see Modelling Cake Toppers)

The elephant

THE DRUMS

1. **To make the drums** for the elephant and the seal bases you will need 134g (4¾oz) of white modelling paste, equally divided. Roll each piece a fat sausage shape and flatten with your hand then push a 4cm (1½in) circle cutter into the paste. Each drum should measure 2 x 4cm (¾ x 1½in) (**A**).

2. **To make the drum top** roll out 16g (⅝oz) of blue sugarpaste, cut out two 4cm (1½in) circles with the cutter (**A**) and attach to the top of the drum.

3. **To complete the flags for both drums** you will need 6g (⅛oz) each of yellow, blue and red sugarpaste and 3g (⅛oz) of green sugarpaste. Roll out the yellow, blue and red sugarpaste into strips measuring 2 x 7cm (¾ x 2¾in) and cut out four triangles from each strip (**A**). Roll out the green sugarpaste into a strip measuring 2 x 3.5cm (¾ x 1⅜in) and cut out two triangles. Attach the flags alternatively around the drum.

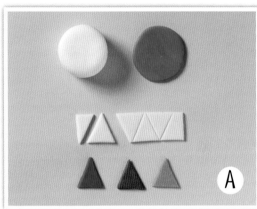

THE BODY AND LEGS

1. **To make the body** you will need 17g (⅝oz) of grey sugarpaste with CMC (Tylose) added, rolled into a cone shape (**B**). Place the cone in the centre of the drum then push a piece of dry spaghetti down through the centre, leaving 2cm (¾in) showing at the top. Push two short pieces of dry spaghetti into the sides of the cone to take the front legs.

2. **To make the back legs** you will need 6g (⅛oz) of grey sugarpaste with CMC added. Roll into a short sausage shape and make a diagonal cut in the centre. Flatten the ends of the legs with your fingers and attach to the base of the body, turning them outwards (**B**).

3. **For the front legs** repeat Step 2 using 4g (⅛oz) of grey sugarpaste with CMC added and attaching to the upper part of the body (**B**).

4. **For the pink tongue and toes** take off a tiny amount from 1g (⅛oz) of fuchsia pink sugarpaste to make a small cone shape for the tongue and insert inside the mouth. Make four small balls from the fuchsia sugarpaste and attach to each foot, pressing them on and flattening them with your finger (**B**).

5. **To make the tail** you will need 1g (⅛oz) of grey sugarpaste rolled into a tapered cone shape. Make a diagonal cut at the thickest end and using tool no.4, feather the other end of the tail by marking it with downward strokes (**B**). Attach to the back of the elephant.

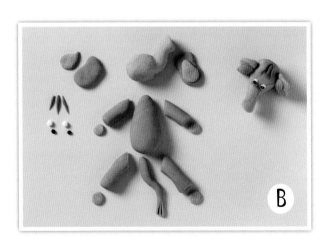

THE HEAD

1. **To complete the head** you will need 15g (½oz) of grey sugarpaste with CMC added, rolled into a ball. Place the ball onto the work surface and using your finger, roll out half of it to make a trunk (**B**). Make a curve in the trunk and push the end of tool no.1 inside to form a hole. Use the edge of a 2cm (¾in) circle cutter to mark a smile and open the mouth using the soft end of your paintbrush.

2. **For the eyes** take off enough from 1g (⅛oz) of white modelling paste to make two small balls and place them close together just above the trunk. From 1g (⅛oz) of black sugarpaste, roll two very small balls for the pupils (**B**) and press them onto the eyeballs.

3. **For the ears** you will need 4g (⅛oz) of grey sugarpaste with CMC added, equally divided and rolled into two small sausage shapes. Flatten the shapes with your fingers, making them wider at the base than at the top (**B**). Line the ears with 2g (⅛oz) of fuchsia pink sugarpaste, equally divided, rolling the same shapes in a smaller size and attaching to the insides of the ears. Push short pieces of dry spaghetti into the sides of the head and slip the ears over the top, securing them with edible glue.

TIP *Highlight the eyes with a cocktail stick (toothpick) dipped into some white edible paint.*

The seal

THE BODY AND FINS

1. **To complete the seal's body** you will need 30g (1⅛oz) of grey sugarpaste with CMC added, rolled into a tapered cone shape. Flatten the tail with your finger and divide then mark the fins using tool no.4 (**C**).

C

2. **Shape the neck** with your fingers, reducing the thickness and keeping the head rounded. Shape the body into a curve, keeping the head and tail upward (**C**). Push a piece of dry spaghetti into the drum and secure the centre of the body over the top.

3. **Roll two fins** using 5g (⅛oz) of grey sugarpaste, equally divided and rolled into two tapered cone shapes (**C**). Flatten with your fingers and attach to each side of the body.

ADDING THE FEATURES

1. **Make two fat cheeks** using 2g (⅛oz) of grey sugarpaste mixed with 1g (⅛oz) of white modelling paste to create a lighter shade. Equally divide the sugarpaste and roll into two fat cone shapes. Attach the pointed ends to the centre of the face and mark the whiskers with the rounded end of tool no.4 (**C**).

2. **For the lower jaw** roll a small oval shape from 1g (⅛oz) of grey sugarpaste and attach under the

cheeks. Take off a small amount from 1g (⅛oz) of fuchsia pink sugarpaste, roll an oval shape for the tongue and attach between the jaw and the centre of the cheeks (**C**).

3. **To make the eyes** take off enough from 1g (⅛oz) of black sugarpaste to roll two small balls and attach just above the cheeks. Roll a cone shape from black sugarpaste for the nose and secure between the tops of the cheeks (**C**).

The tent

THE BASE

1. **To make the base** you will need 105g (3⅞oz) of white modelling paste. Roll into a fat sausage shape measuring 5cm (2in) in height, keeping the paste smooth. Push a piece of dry spaghetti through the centre, leaving 4cm (1¾in) showing at the top. Roll out 35g (1¼oz) of red sugarpaste, cut out four stripes measuring 1.5 x 6cm (⅝ x 2⅜in) (**D**) and attach evenly around the base.

2. **To make the top** roll 47g (1¾oz) of white modelling paste into a cone shape measuring 7cm (2¾in) in height. Flatten the cone at the bottom and use your fingers to spread it out to make it wider than the base. Make eight stripes using 16g (⅝oz) of red sugarpaste and 16g (⅝oz) of white modelling paste. Take off 4g (⅛oz) for each stripe and roll into a tapered sausage shape measuring 7cm (2¾in) in length. Widen and flatten the shapes with a rolling pin and arrange alternately around the top. Slip the completed top over the spaghetti in the base. From 1g (⅛oz) of red sugarpaste, roll a ball and attach on top of the tent (**D**).

THE FLAGS

To make the tape roll out 2g (⅛oz) of red sugarpaste and cut out a strip measuring 7 x 0.3cm (2¾ x ⅛in). For the flags you will need 1g (⅛oz) of red, blue, green and yellow sugarpaste with CMC added, cut into 1.2cm (½in) squares. Cut the squares diagonally, attach a triangle from each colour to the tape (**D**) and secure to the front of the tent.

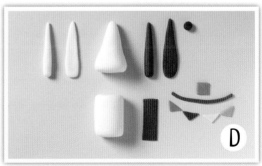

TIP *It is easier to attach the strip to the front of the tent first and then hang the flags on top.*

My Easter Bunny

*Poppy is a contented little girl who has had all her Easter wishes come true!
A soft and snuggly toy bunny to cherish as well as a delicious chocolate egg,
wrapped in pretty pink polka dot foil and tied in a beautiful red bow.*

You will need:

Sugarpaste

- 72g (2⅝oz) flesh
- 51g (1¾oz) grey
- 49g (1¾oz) yellow
- 31g (1⅛oz) black
- 28g (1⅛oz) pink
- 6g (⅛oz) fuchsia
- 1g (⅛oz) dark blue

Materials

- 90g (3¼oz) white modelling paste
- White vegetable fat (shortening)
- CMC (Tylose)
- Sugarflair liquid food colour in blue and black
- Edible glue

Equipment

- 3cm (1¼in), 7cm (2¾in), 10cm (4in) circle cutters
- 6mm (¼in), 1cm (⅜in) oval cutters
- Fine paintbrush no. 0000
- Cocktail stick (toothpick)
- Frilling tool (optional)
- Basic tool kit (see Modelling Cake Toppers)

Poppy

POPPY'S BODY, ARMS AND LEGS

1. **To make the body** you will need 50g (1¾oz) of white modelling paste rolled into a cone shape (**A**). Place the cone onto a cake card then push a piece of dry spaghetti down through the centre of the body.

2. **For the legs** you will need 38g (1⅜oz) of flesh sugarpaste with CMC (Tylose) added. Roll the sugarpaste into a sausage shape and make a diagonal cut in the centre to make two legs. Narrow each piece around the ankles and indent the backs of the knees (**A**). Push a short piece of dry spaghetti into the hipline of each leg and attach to the body, keeping the knees bent. Push a further piece of dry spaghetti into the bottom of each leg.

3. **To make the shoes** take 10g (¼oz) of pastel yellow sugarpaste and equally divide. Roll each piece into a ball then into a cone shape to form the shoes (**A**). Take off enough from 3g (⅛oz) of white modelling paste to make two small balls then flatten and attach to the top of each shoe. Slip the shoes over the spaghetti at the base of the legs.

TIP *To prevent the modelling paste from sticking to the cake card, dust with cornflour or icing (confectioners') sugar first. Support the knees underneath with foam until dry.*

4. **For the sock tops** thinly roll out the remaining white modelling paste, cut out two strips, each measuring 1.5 x 4cm (⅝ x 1½in) (**A**) and attach with edible glue.

5. **To make the arms** you will need 10g (¼oz) of flesh sugarpaste with CMC added. Make a sausage shape and divide with a diagonal cut in the centre. Narrow each arm, shape at the wrists and indent the insides of the

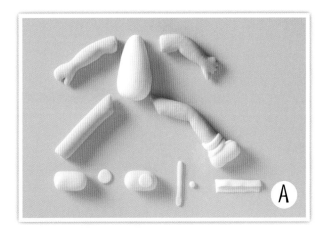

elbows. Flatten the palms of the hands a little with your finger and take out the thumbs. Round off the edges and indent four fingers with tool no.4. Bend each arm at the elbow and make a straight cut, 1cm (⅜in) up from each elbow. Set aside and keep covered until required (**A**).

THE CLOTHING

1. **For the petticoats** thinly roll out 16g (⅝oz) of white modelling paste and cut out two circles with a 10cm (4in) cutter. Using the end of your paintbrush or a frilling tool, frill the edges all around the circles as shown (**B**) then remove the centres with a 3cm (1¼in) round cutter. Slip the petticoats over the spaghetti at the top of the body and arrange them around the top of the legs.

2. **To make the dress** you will need 23g (⅞oz) of pastel yellow sugarpaste, rolled out. Use a cutter to take out a 10cm (4in) circle (**B**). Apply some edible glue around the upper body then place the circle over the spaghetti at the neck. Do not pull the shape down but gently press it in to the upper body, leaving the skirt to flow openly over the petticoats from the waistline down. Push a short piece of dry spaghetti into the shoulders on either side.

3. **To make the sleeves** you will need 12g (⅜oz) of yellow sugarpaste equally divided and rolled into two balls. Slip each piece over the spaghetti at the shoulder line and push a further piece of dry spaghetti into the base of each sleeve. Take off enough from 1g (⅛oz) of yellow sugarpaste to roll two thin laces and attach around the base of the sleeves (**B**). You do not need to add the arms to the sleeves until the bunny is completed.

4. **For the collar** roll out 6g (⅛oz) of white modelling paste and cut into a rectangle measuring 4.5 x 3.2cm (1¾ x 1¼in) (**B**). Make stitch marks around the edges using tool no.12 and place the collar centrally over the spaghetti at the neck.

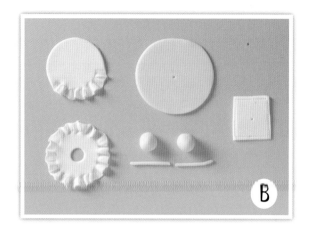

TIP Mark the centre of each circle to ensure it will be placed centrally over the spaghetti at the neck. Arrange the folds as necessary with the soft end of your paintbrush.

THE HEAD

1. **For Poppy's head** you will need 24g (1oz) of flesh sugarpaste with CMC added, rolled into a ball. Pull down the neck from underneath the ball then indent the eye area with your little finger (**C**). Make a straight cut at the base of the neck – the leftover paste will be used for the ears and nose. Place the head into an upright position inside a flower former.

2. **For the nose** roll a tiny ball of flesh sugarpaste into an oval shape and place in the centre of the face. Mark a large smile beneath the nose using the smiley tool no.11 (**C**). Using the soft end of your paintbrush, level out the top lip and open up the mouth a little.

3. **To make the eyes** take off enough from 1g (⅛oz) of white modelling paste to make two small eyeballs. Place them just above and to either side of the nose and flatten with your finger. Take some blue liquid food colour and paint on the irises with a small brush. Clean the brush and use it to remove some of the paint from the centres, making them a pale blue shade. Use black liquid food colour and a small brush to add small pupils, fine eyelashes and eyebrows (**C**).

TIP *Remember that when you flatten out the eyeballs, they will increase in size.*

4. **To make the lips** take off a tiny amount from 1g (⅛oz) of pink sugarpaste. Roll into thin banana shapes for the top and bottom lips and position in place (**C**).

5. **For the ears** use the leftover flesh sugarpaste to roll two small cone shapes and attach to either side of the head (**C**). Use your paintbrush to indent the lower part of the ears. Place the head over the spaghetti at the top of the body, tilting it to one side.

THE HAIR AND BOWS

1. **To make the hair** soften 30g (1⅛oz) of black sugarpaste with white vegetable fat (shortening). Take off 10g (¼oz) and roll into a ball. Using your fingers, open out the ball to make a cap large enough to fit the head (**C**). Apply some edible glue around the head and place the cap into position. Using the rounded end of tool no.4, make a parting line down the centre back of the head and mark the hairlines from the centre to the side.

2. **To make the curls** fill the cup of a sugar press (or garlic press) and extrude long strands. Take off three at a time and twist them together (**C**) then attach them to either side of the head.

3. **Make the fringe** by extruding shorter lengths of hair, as in Step 2. Arrange in a line over the top of the head, falling over the forehead (**C**).

4. **To make two hair bows** you will need 3g (⅛oz) of pastel yellow sugarpaste. Take off enough to make two small cone shapes then flatten them with your finger. Place the points together at the top of the curls, add a small ball in the centre then mark on the crease lines with tool no.4 (**C**).

Easter bunny

THE BODY

1. **To make the bunny's body** you will need 21g (¾oz) of light grey sugarpaste with CMC added, rolled into a cone shape (**D**). Place onto Poppy's knee and secure with edible glue. Keeping the body upright, push a piece of dry spaghetti down through the centre, leaving 2cm (¾in) showing at the top.

2. **For the white chest patch** you will need 2g (⅛oz) of white modelling paste rolled into a flattened cone shape measuring 4 x 2cm (2¼ x ¾in) wide. Attach to the centre front of the body (**D**).

3. **For the back legs** you will need 12g (⅜oz) of light grey sugarpaste equally divided. Roll each piece into a fat cone shape (**D**) then attach to each side of body.

4. **To make the feet** you will need a further 6g (⅛oz) of light grey sugarpaste divided equally. Roll each piece into a fat cone shape, slightly flatten with your fingers (**D**) then attach to the base of the back legs.

TIP *When making the body shaped cone for the Easter Bunny, give him a nicely rounded tummy.*

THE HEAD

1. **For the head** roll 8g (¼oz) of light grey sugarpaste into a ball and slightly indent the eye area with your finger (**D**). Place the head into a flower former and insert two short pieces of dry spaghetti for the ears.

2. **To complete the ears** you will need 4g (⅛oz) of grey sugarpaste, equally divided and each piece rolled into a tapered cone shape. Indent the inside of both ears with the handle of your paintbrush. Make a pink lining by rolling two tapered cone shapes taken from 1g (⅛oz) of pink sugarpaste (**D**). Secure to the centre of each ear with glue, slip the ears over the spaghetti on the head and set the pink sugarpaste aside.

3. **For the facial characteristics** take 4g (⅛oz) of white modelling paste for the cheeks and equally divide. Roll each piece into a fat cone shape and attach the points to the centre of the face. Take off enough from 1g (⅛oz) of pink sugarpaste to make a small oval shape for the lower lip. From the leftover pink sugarpaste, roll a small, flattened circle for the tongue and place on top of the lower lip. Add a small pink sugarpaste cone shape for the nose and place in-between the tip of the cheeks (**D**). Mark the cheeks with three dots using a cocktail stick (toothpick).

4. **For the eyes** roll out the remaining white modelling paste and using a 1cm (⅜in) oval cutter, take out two shapes. Place in an upright position just above and on either side of the nose. Cut out two smaller 6mm (¼in) oval shapes for the irises from 1g (⅛oz) of dark blue sugarpaste and place on top of the white eyeballs. From 1g (⅛oz) of black sugarpaste, roll two small black pupils and place on top of the irises (**D**).

5. Apply some edible glue around the top of the body and slip the head over the spaghetti at the top.

ARMS AND PAWS

1. **Attach Poppy's arms** (see Step 5 of Poppy's body, arms and legs) to the sleeves and bring them around the front of the rabbit.

2. **To make the bunny's front paws** you will need 8g (¼oz) of white modelling paste, equally divided and rolled into two fat cone shapes. Attach the left paw over Poppy's left arm and the right paw underneath her right arm. Indent the paw marks using tool no.4 (**D**).

Easter egg

1. **To make the egg** roll 25g (1oz) of pale pink sugarpaste with CMC added into an egg shape (**E**).

2. **To complete the ribbon** roll out 6g (⅛oz) of fuchsia pink sugarpaste and cut a strip measuring 1.5 x 7cm (⅝ x 2¾in) (**E**). Mark the ribbon down each side with the stitch-marking tool no.12. Apply edible glue around the egg and place the ribbon over the top, trimming off any excess.

3. **To make the bow** cut out a further strip measuring 1.5 x 8cm (⅝ x 3¼in). Apply some glue to the centre of the strip then fold over the ends into the centre, making two loops. Turn the bow over and pinch the raw edges underneath (**E**). Mark the top of the bow in the centre with tool no.4 and attach to the top of the egg.

4. Use any leftover fuchsia pink sugarpaste to make tiny dots of different sizes to decorate the egg (**E**).

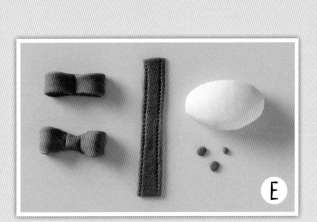

E

Enchanted Garden

This enchanting garden scene features a friendly snail with a colourful shell, a cheeky little caterpillar and a charming toadstool house – the perfect pixie dwelling place. It is sure appeal to any child's imagination and will add magic to their special day!

You will need:

Sugarpaste

- 94g (3⅜oz) pastel green
- 88g (3⅛oz) pastel yellow
- 87g (3⅛oz) grey
- 77g (2⅞oz) fuchsia pink
- 33g (1¼oz) dark green
- 27g (1⅛oz) pink
- 16g (½oz) duck egg blue
- 16g (½oz) lime green
- 10g (¼oz) orange
- 6g (⅛oz) teddy bear brown
- 1g (⅛oz) black

Materials

- 8g (¼oz) white modelling paste
- White vegetable fat (shortening)
- CMC (Tylose)
- Edible white paint or white paste food colour
- Edible food pens in brown and pink
- Edible glue

Equipment

- 10cm (4in) round silver cake card
- 2.5cm (1in) oval cutter
- 13mm (⅝in) square cutter
- 2.5mm (⅛in), 6mm (¼in), 1cm (⅜in), 12mm (½in), 3cm (1¼in) circle cutters
- 12mm (½in) blossom cutter
- Cocktail stick (toothpick)
- Basic tool kit (see Modelling Cake Toppers)

Snail

THE BODY

1. **To make the body** you will need 45g (1⅝oz) of pastel yellow sugarpaste with CMC (Tylose) added. Roll into a fat cone shape with the pointed end at the back of the snail. Pull out two feet at the front of the body then pull up some sugarpaste to form the neck (**A**). Spread out the edges of the body with your finger to flatten both sides. Push a piece of dry spaghetti into the neck, leaving 2cm (¾in) showing to support the head.

2. **For the base of the shell** add some CMC to 20g (¾oz) of pastel yellow sugarpaste and roll into an oval shape (**A**). Arch it a little and attach over the spaghetti in the centre of the snail's back.

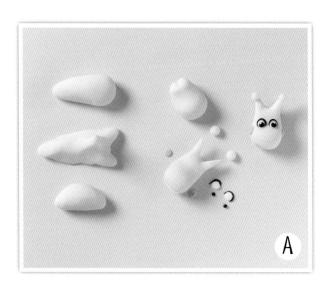

THE HEAD

1. **To make the head** you will need 16g (½oz) of pastel yellow sugarpaste with CMC added. Narrow the top third of the shape by indenting with your fingers, keeping the lower part of the shape very round (**A**).

2. **To form a smile** press the edge of a 3cm (1¼in) circle cutter into the mouth area. When dry, outline the smile with a pink edible food pen (**A**).

3. **To make the antennae** indent the centre top of the head with your paintbrush and pull up two narrow cone shapes. Carefully push a short piece of dry spaghetti through the top of each one then roll two small balls (**A**) from 1g (⅛oz) of pastel yellow sugarpaste and attach on top.

TIP *When pressing the edge of the cutter into the head to make the smile, be sure to place it high enough so that it can be seen.*

4. **To make the cheeks** roll out 1g (⅛oz) of pink sugarpaste and use a cutter to cut out two 6mm (¼in) circles (**A**). Attach to either side of the head.

5. **For the eyes** take off enough from 1g (⅛oz) of white modelling paste to make two small balls and outline with a fine lace taken from 1g (⅛oz) of black sugarpaste. Roll two tiny black sugarpaste balls for the pupils and press onto each eyeball (**A**). Roll a tiny dot of white modelling paste to highlight each eye and slip the completed head over the spaghetti at the neck.

THE SHELL

1. **To complete the shell** you will need 10g (¼oz) each of duck egg blue, orange, pastel green and dark green sugarpaste and 20g (¾oz) of pale pink sugarpaste. Apply some edible glue all over the back of the snail. Take 10g (¼oz) from the pale pink sugarpaste, roll into a tapered cone shape and place at the back of the snail (**B**).

2. Roll the orange, duck egg blue, pink and pastel green shapes into tapered cone shapes and add, making the tips meet in the centre. Finally roll the dark green sugarpaste into a longer tapered shape (**B**) and attach close to the snail's head.

3. **Make the central flower** by rolling out 3g (⅛oz) of dark green sugarpaste and pressing out the shape with a 12mm (½in) blossom cutter. Indent each petal with the end of your paintbrush and roll a tiny ball of each of the colours to attach in each indented circle. Repeat to make a flower for each side of the snail and attach with edible glue.

TIP *Adjust the length of each colour to fit snugly over the top of the cone-shaped base and link into each other, keeping a dome shape at the top.*

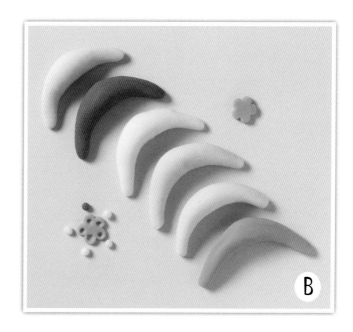

B

Caterpillar

1. **To complete the caterpillar** you will need 16g (½oz) of lime green sugarpaste with CMC added. Take off 15g (½oz) and roll it into a long sausage shape, measuring 8cm (3¼in) in length. Narrow the neck area by rolling with your little finger on the work surface, leaving the rounded top for the head (**C**).

2. **To make the front legs** use the remaining 1g (⅛oz) of lime green sugarpaste to roll two small sausage shapes (**C**) and attach to the body.

3. **For the antennae** roll a tiny lace from lime green sugarpaste, curl at the ends (**C**) and attach to the top of the head.

4. **For the underbelly** roll 6g (⅛oz) of pastel yellow sugarpaste with CMC added into a slightly smaller sausage shape. Attach underneath the body then shape the caterpillar by lifting up the front end. Using the rounded end of tool no.4, mark horizontal lines across the underbelly. Make some tiny spots from 1g (⅛oz) of pastel yellow sugarpaste and attach to the top of the body (**C**).

5. **Add the facial features** firstly using the smiley tool no.11 to mark the mouth. Roll two small eyeballs from 1g (⅛oz) of white modelling paste and press them in place. Add two tiny black sugarpaste balls for the pupils (**C**) and highlight the eyes with a cocktail stick (toothpick) dipped into some white edible paint or white paste food colour.

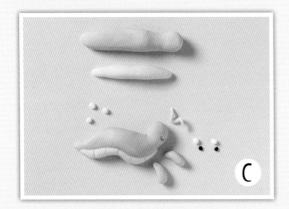

C

Toadstool house and garden

THE GARDEN

To complete the garden base you will need an 84g (3oz) ball of pastel green sugarpaste, rolled out to make an irregular shape measuring 10cm (4in) in width (**D**). Place the base over a 10cm (4in) round silver cake card covered with edible glue, allowing the edges of the paste to flow over the sides to hide the card.

TIP *Working the sugarpaste in this way will give a much softer edge than if you use a 10cm (4in) circle cutter.*

THE TOADSTOOL HOUSE

1. **To make the base** you will need 75g (2¾oz) of grey sugarpaste mixed well with CMC. Shape the sugarpaste into a fat cone shape (**D**) and place on the garden, leaving a finger's width from the back. Push a length of dry spaghetti down through the centre, leaving 4cm (2¾in) showing at the top.

TIP *It is important to keep the base of the house upright until it is dry.*

2. **To make the roof** you will need 75g (2¾oz) of fuchsia pink sugarpaste with CMC added. Roll into a cone shape (**D**) and hollow out the centre a little with your fingers to make the top overhang the base.

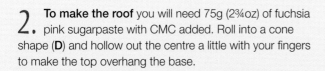

3. **For the chimney** you will need 4g (⅛oz) of grey sugarpaste with CMC added, rolled into a small cone shape (**D**). Make a diagonal cut at the widest end so that it fits neatly onto the roof. Push a short piece of dry spaghetti down through the centre, leaving 1cm (⅜in) showing at the top.

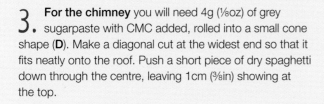

4. **For the chimney top** roll 2g (⅛oz) of fuchsia pink sugarpaste into a cone shape and hollow out a little with your finger and thumb (**D**). Slip the top over the base and attach the chimney to the side of the roof.

5. **For the spots** thinly roll out 4g (⅛oz) of white modelling paste, use cutters to cut out six 12mm (½in) and three 6mm (¼in) circles (**D**) and attach around the top of the roof.

6. **To make the step** roll out 3g (⅛in) of grey sugarpaste to a 5mm (¼in) thickness and cut out a square using a 13mm square cutter (**D**). Attach to the base of the house at the centre front.

7. **To make the door** roll out 3g (⅛oz) of pink sugarpaste, cut out an oval shape using a 2.5cm (1in) oval cutter and make a straight edge at the bottom. Mark two vertical lines down the door with tool no.4 then attach to the centre front of the house, directly over the step. Roll 2g (⅛oz) of duck egg blue sugarpaste into a thin lace and attach in an arched shape for the doorframe. From 1g (⅛oz) of white modeling paste, roll a tiny ball for the doorknob, add to the door (**D**) and set the remaining white paste aside.

8. **For the window** roll out 2g (⅛oz) of white modelling paste, use a cutter to cut out a 1cm (⅜in) circle and attach to the side of the house. Roll out a further 2g (⅛oz) of duck egg blue sugarpaste and cut out a 12mm (½in) circle with a cutter. Take out the centre with a 1cm (⅜in) circle cutter and place over the window to make the window frame (**D**). When the sugarpaste is dry, mark the frame with a brown edible food pen.

THE GRASS AND STONE PATH

1. **To form the grass** soften 20g (¾oz) of dark green sugarpaste with white vegetable fat (shortening) and fill the cup of the sugar press (or garlic press). Extrude some short strands and take them off in a clump (**D**) to arrange around the house.

2. **For the stone path** you will need 6g (⅛oz) of teddy bear brown sugarpaste, rolled into small balls. Flatten with your finger (**D**) and lace the balls side-by-side to create the pathway. Add some additional stones on either side of the garden and mark spots onto the stones with a brown edible food pen.

THE SMALL TOADSTOOLS

1. **For the blue toadstool** roll 3g (⅛oz) of grey sugarpaste into a cone shape for the stalk (**D**). To make the top roll 2g (⅛oz) of duck egg blue sugarpaste into a cone shape, hollow out a little with tool no.1 and attach to the top of the stalk. Secure the blue toadstool to the side of the large toadstool house. From the remaining white sugarpaste, roll a small ball and press it on to the top of the blue top.

2. **For the pink toadstool** repeat Step 1, using 2g (⅛oz) of grey sugarpaste for the stalk and 1g (⅛oz) of pink sugarpaste for the top. Position in front of the blue mushroom and add some dots around the top using a brown edible food pen (**D**).

TIP *The small mushrooms will not require any CMC or spaghetti as they are so small.*

Farmer Tom's Tractor

No farm is complete without a big red tractor! As soon as the animals hear the noise of the engine, they know their friend Farmer Tom is not far away. Boys of all ages with love this charming topper.

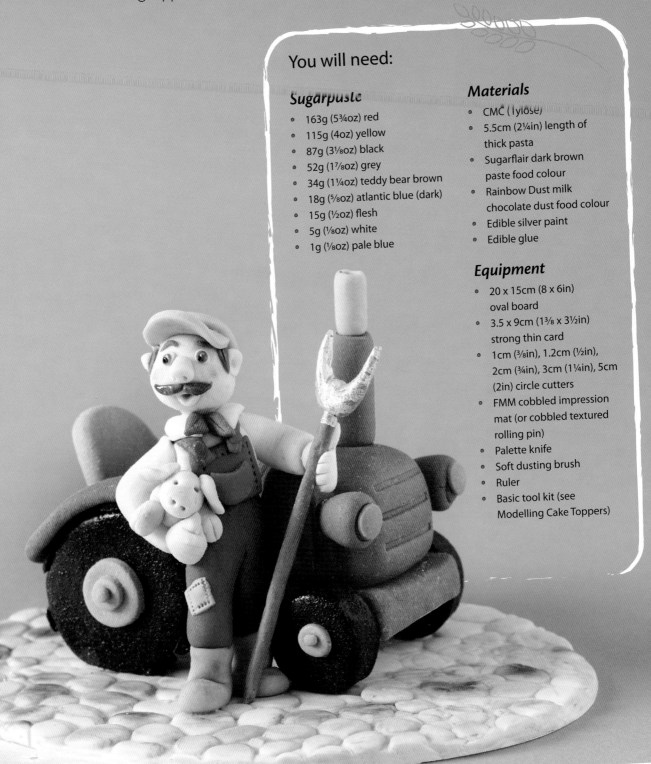

You will need:

Sugarpaste

- 163g (5¾oz) red
- 115g (4oz) yellow
- 87g (3⅛oz) black
- 52g (1⅞oz) grey
- 34g (1¼oz) teddy bear brown
- 18g (⅝oz) atlantic blue (dark)
- 15g (½oz) flesh
- 5g (⅛oz) white
- 1g (⅛oz) pale blue

Materials

- CMC (Tylose)
- 5.5cm (2¼in) length of thick pasta
- Sugarflair dark brown paste food colour
- Rainbow Dust milk chocolate dust food colour
- Edible silver paint
- Edible glue

Equipment

- 20 x 15cm (8 x 6in) oval board
- 3.5 x 9cm (1⅜ x 3½in) strong thin card
- 1cm (⅜in), 1.2cm (½in), 2cm (¾in), 3cm (1¼in), 5cm (2in) circle cutters
- FMM cobbled impression mat (or cobbled textured rolling pin)
- Palette knife
- Soft dusting brush
- Ruler
- Basic tool kit (see Modelling Cake Toppers)

Big red tractor

THE COBBLED YARD

1. **For the cobbled yard** you will need to cover a 20 x 15cm (8 x 6in) oval board with 100g (4oz) of yellow sugarpaste mixed randomly with 20g (¾oz) of teddy bear brown sugarpaste, rolled out to a 5mm (¼in) thickness. Place the sugarpaste over the board then use either a cobbled textured rolling pin or an impression mat to roll over the top.

2. Trim around the edges with a palette knife and dust over the surface with milk chocolate dust food colour.

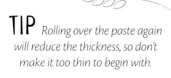

TIP *Rolling over the paste again will reduce the thickness, so don't make it too thin to begin with.*

THE TRACTOR BASE

1. **To make the base** you will need 60g (2¼oz) of red sugarpaste with plenty of CMC (Tylose) added to give it strength. Knead the sugarpaste well then roll it out to measure 1 x 4.5 x 10cm (⅜ x 1¾ x 4in) (**A**).

2. Apply some glue over the surface of the 3.5 x 9cm (1⅜ x 3½in) strong thin card. Place the sugarpaste base over the card and lay a 5.5cm (2¼in) length of thick pasta across the ends of the base to support the large wheels. Leave on a flat surface to dry.

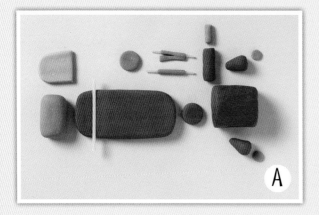

THE SEAT

1. **To make the seat** add some CMC to 30g (1⅛oz) of grey sugarpaste. Take off 20g (¾oz) and mould into an oblong shape measuring 4.5 x 2cm (1¾ x ¾in) (**A**). Place the seat 5mm (¼in) from the end of the base, covering the pasta and pushing it down firmly.

2. **Make the back of the seat** using 10g (¼oz) of grey sugarpaste rolled into a sausage shape. Using a rolling pin, widen the shape to measure 3 x 4.5cm (1¼ x 1¾in). Keeping the rounded end for the top, make a straight cut at the bottom (**A**) and attach to the base and back of the seat.

THE ENGINE

1. **For the engine** take 66g (2⅜oz) of red sugarpaste and add some CMC. Roll into a ball, use your fingers to shape into a 4cm (1½in) squared off shape and attach to the front of the base, 5mm (¼in) from the front (**A**).

2. Mark three horizontal lines on the front of the radiator and three vertical lines on each side of the grill using the end of a ruler.

THE CHIMNEY

1. **For the chimney** you will need 6g (⅛oz) of red sugarpaste with CMC added, rolled into a sausage shape measuring 3.5cm (1⅜in) in length (**A**). Place the chimney on the side of the engine then push a piece of dry spaghetti down through the centre and into the engine, leaving 3cm (1¼in) showing at the top.

2. **Make the funnel** using 1g (⅛oz) of grey sugarpaste with CMC added, rolled into a thin sausage shape (**A**). Slip the funnel over the spaghetti at the top of the chimney and make a hole in the top with the pokey tool no.5.

THE HEADLIGHTS

1. **For the headlights** you will need 5g (⅛oz) of red sugarpaste with CMC added equally divided, with each piece rolled into a fat cone shape. Roll out 1g (⅛oz) of grey sugarpaste, cut out two 1cm (⅜in) circles for the glass (**A**) and attach in the centre of each cone.

2. Push a short piece of dry spaghetti into the sides of the engine where the lights are to be positioned then secure them in place.

THE DASHBOARD

1. **For the dashboard** roll out 4g (⅛oz) of red sugarpaste to a 5mm (¼in) thickness, use a cutter to take out a 2cm (¾in) circle (**A**) and attach to the engine.

2. **To complete the steering wheel** you will need 3g (⅛oz) of grey sugarpaste. To make the steering column, take off 1g (⅛oz) and roll out thinly. Cut a 1.5cm (⅝in) square and run a line of glue in the centre. Place a piece of dry spaghetti over the glue and fold the sugarpaste over the top (**A**). Trim off the sugarpaste close to the spaghetti with tool no.4 and roll out on the work surface to thin it out. Push the end of the spaghetti into the centre of the dashboard.

3. **To make the steering wheel** roll out the remaining grey sugarpaste and cut out a 3cm (1¼in) circle. Attach over the spaghetti at the end of the steering column to complete (**A**).

THE WHEELS

1. **For the back wheels** you will need 68g (2⅜oz) of black sugarpaste with a level teaspoon of CMC added, kneaded well and rolled out to a 13mm (½in) thickness. Take out two circles with a 5cm (2in) cutter (**B**) and place them on a flat surface.

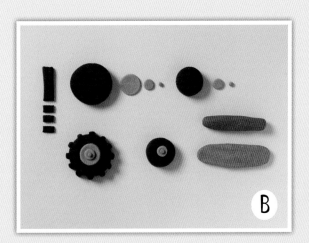

2. **To make the treads** roll out the leftover black sugarpaste from the back tyres to a 3mm (⅛in) thickness. Cut some 5mm (¼in) wide strips and cut again into small rectangular shapes, measuring them to fit across the tyre (**B**).

3. **To complete the front wheels** you will need 18g (⅝oz) of black sugarpaste with CMC added. Roll out to a thickness of 1cm (⅜in) then take out two circles with a 3cm (1¼in) cutter (**B**) and place on a flat surface.

4. **For the wheel discs** roll out 6g (⅛oz) of grey sugarpaste to a 2mm (¹⁄₁₆in) thickness then take out two circles using a 2cm (¾in) cutter and four circles using a 1cm (⅜in) cutter (**B**).

5. Attach the larger circles to the centre of the back tyres, place the smaller circles inside and add a small round ball of grey sugarpaste into the centre. Repeat for the front tyres using the two smaller circles (**B**).

6. Slip the back wheels over the pasta at the back of the tractor. To attach the front wheels, push a piece of dry spaghetti right through the base and attach the wheels over the top. Press the wheels against the side of the base for more support.

7. **To complete the mudguards** you will need 22g (⅞oz) of red sugarpaste with CMC added, equally divided. Roll each piece into a sausage shape and widen with your rolling pin (**B**). Attach the mudguard over each back wheel.

Farmer Tom

THE BODY, ARMS AND LEGS

1. **To make the lower body and legs** you will need 16g (½oz) of atlantic blue (dark) sugarpaste with CMC added, rolled into a small cone shape. Flatten the shape a little with your hand, keeping the widest end at the base. Using tool no.4, push the point into the centre of the shape and equally divide for the legs (**C**). Using your fingers, round off all of the straight edges and flatten the end of each leg.

2. **For the patch on the trouser leg** cut out a 1cm (⅜in) square from 1g (⅛oz) of pale blue sugarpaste (**C**). Secure to the trousers and edge using the stitch-marking tool no.12. The trouser legs will finish just above the knee.

3. **Make the upper body** by rolling 7g (¼oz) of yellow sugarpaste with CMC added into a small fat cone shape (**C**) and attaching to the lower body.

C

4. **To make the wellington boots** roll 7g (¼oz) of teddy bear brown sugarpaste with CMC added into a sausage shape. Turn up the rounded ends with the flat of your index finger to shape the feet, adjusting the length of the boots if necessary. Make a straight cut at the centre and slip the boots over the spaghetti at the end of each leg (**C**).

5. Take a piece of dry spaghetti, taller than the height of the body and push it down from the neck, through one leg and into the foot. Repeat for the other side and break off any spaghetti showing at the top of the body. Let the figure stand supported from the back until it has dried a little, then stand it beside the tractor.

6. **To complete the arms** you will need 7g (¼oz) of yellow sugarpaste with CMC added, rolled into a sausage shape. Make a diagonal cut in the centre and bend at each elbow (**C**). Push a short piece of dry spaghetti into each shoulder and slip the arms over the top. One arm will be resting on the tractor and the other on the farmer's hip, leaving enough room for a small pig. Push a short piece of dry spaghetti into the end of each wrist.

7. **To make the hands** you will need 1g (⅛oz) of flesh sugarpaste, equally divided. Roll each piece into a small cone shape and flatten with your finger. Using tool no.4, mark out the thumb and round off the edges. Mark four knuckles by indenting the top of the hand with tool no.4. Slip the right hand over the spaghetti at the wrist – this will be secured to the pig. Attach the left hand to the arm resting on the tractor, leaving the palm open to attach the pitchfork to later (**C**).

THE BIB, BRACES AND COLLAR

1. **To make the bib** thinly roll out 2g (⅛oz) of atlantic blue (dark) sugarpaste and cut out a 1.5cm (⅝in) square piece. Mark stitches around three sides with tool no.12 and attach to the centre of the body. Make a small pocket from the same sugarpaste using a 1.2cm (½in) circle cutter. Take out a third of the shape with the edge of the circle cutter to curve the top of the pocket then attach to the bib (**C**).

2. **For the braces** roll out the remaining blue sugarpaste and cut out two narrow strips. Attach one end to the top of the bib and the other end over the shoulders, then cross over at the back (**C**).

3. **To make the collar** roll out 1g (⅛oz) of yellow sugarpaste and cut out a 1.5cm (⅝in) square. Divide the centre front then make a diagonal cut across each corner. Place the collar over the spaghetti at the neck and make a division in the centre back.

THE HEAD AND CAP

1. **To complete the head** you will need 8g (¼oz) of flesh sugarpaste with CMC added. Take off 7g (¼oz), knead well and roll into a smooth ball. Pull down the neck from beneath the ball, twisting with your fingers as you do so. Indent the eye area with your finger then make a straight cut at the base of the neck (**D**).

2. **To make the nose** take off a small amount from the remaining 1g (⅛oz) of flesh sugarpaste and roll into a small cone shape (**D**). Attach to the centre of the face then mark the nostrils with the pokey tool no.5.

3. **Mark the smile** using the smallest end of the smiley tool no.11 then open the mouth with the soft end of a paintbrush. Roll a tiny banana shape from flesh sugarpaste for the bottom lip and attach to the mouth (**D**).

4. **For the ears** roll the remaining flesh sugarpaste into two small cone shapes (**D**), attach to each side of the head and indent the bases with the end of your paintbrush.

5. **To make the eyes** you will need 1g (⅛oz) of white sugarpaste. Take off a very small amount and roll into two balls, place just above and on either side of the nose and flatten slightly with your finger. Make some dark brown sugarpaste by adding some dark brown paste food colour to 4g (⅛oz) of white sugarpaste. Take off enough to make two much smaller balls for the irises, secure them over the eyeballs and set the remaining brown paste aside. From a further 1g (⅛oz) of black sugarpaste, take off two tiny balls for the pupils and place in the centre of the dark brown irises (**D**).

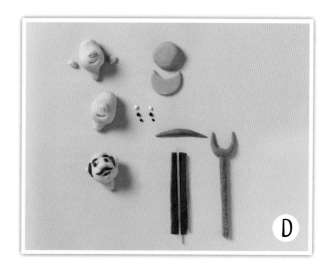

6. **For the sideburns** make two small tapered shapes using the leftover brown sugarpaste and attach to the sides of the face. Roll two very small tapered cone shapes for the moustache and position beneath the nose, curling up at each end. Make two further tiny cone shapes for the eyebrows and arrange above the eyes (**D**).

7. **To complete the cap** you will need 7g (¼oz) of teddy bear brown sugarpaste with CMC added. Take off 4g (⅛oz) and roll into a ball. Using your fingers, open out the shape to fit around the head and secure in place with edible glue. Roll out the remaining sugarpaste, cut out the back of the cap with a 2.5cm (1in) circle cutter and take off a further third of the circle to form a crescent shape (**D**). Apply edible glue to the front of the cap and secure the back in place.

THE PITCHFORK

1. **To complete the pitchfork** you will need 3g (⅛oz) of the leftover dark brown sugarpaste, rolled out to measure 8 x 1cm (3¼ x ⅜in). Run a line of edible glue down the centre and place a length of dry spaghetti over the top. Make the handle as described for the gear stick, leaving 3mm (⅛in) of spaghetti showing at the top (**D**).

2. **For the top of the pitchfork** you will need 1g (⅛oz) of grey sugarpaste. Take off two thirds of the sugarpaste, add some CMC and roll into a tapered sausage shape, curving the ends to form a horseshoe shape. Slip onto the spaghetti at the top of the handle and set aside. Paint the fork with some edible silver paint (**D**).

3. Apply some glue to the right hand and place the pitchfork on top, bringing the thumb and the hand around the handle.

The piglet

1. **To complete the piglet** you will need 3g (⅛oz) of flesh coloured sugarpaste. Take off 1g (⅛oz) and roll into a small cone shape for the body (**E**). Place the pointed end of the cone under the farmers arm and push a short piece of dry spaghetti into the top of the cone.

2. **To make the front legs** take off a further 1g (⅛oz) of flesh coloured sugarpaste and roll into a tiny sausage shape. Make a diagonal cut in the centre then attach to either side of the body. Mark the trotters by making a vertical line with tool no.4 (**E**).

3. **For the head** take off a further 1g (⅛oz) of flesh coloured sugarpaste, roll into a ball and slip it over the spaghetti on the body. Roll a flattened sausage shape for the nose and secure to the centre of the face then make two central nostrils with the pokey tool no.5. Mark two more holes just above for the eyes and with the leftover paste, roll two small flattened cone shapes for the ears and attach to either side of the head (**E**).

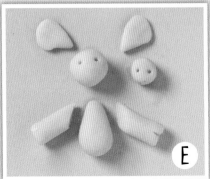

E

Knit One, Purr One

This clever cat would rather curl up on a comfy cushion and knit herself a new snuggly blanket than mindlessly chase after balls of wool with her peers. The purr-fect topper for feline fans and crafty knitters alike!

You will need:

Sugarpaste

- 100g (3½oz) duck egg blue
- 95g (3⅜oz) light grey
- 19g (¾oz) dark blue
- 10g (¼oz) yellow
- 7g (¼oz) white
- 6g (⅛oz) pink
- 5g (⅛oz) lime green
- 1g (⅛oz) dark green
- 1g (⅛oz) black

Materials

- CMC (Tylose)
- White vegetable fat (shortening)
- Edible glue

Equipment

- 2cm (¾in) square cutter
- Crimper
- Basic tool kit (see Modelling Cake Toppers)

The cushion

1. **To make the cushion** you will need 100g (3½oz) of duck egg blue sugarpaste rolled into a soft rectangular shape measuring 8 x 6cm (3¼ x 2¼in). Flatten the shape with your hand to a depth of around 1.5cm (⅝in). Using a crimper, edge the sides all the way around (**A**).

TIP *Using your hands to make the cushion shape will give a much softer look than using a cutter.*

2. **To complete the squares** you will need 5g (⅛oz) each of yellow, lime green and pink sugarpaste. Roll out the coloured sugarpaste and take out two squares in each colour with a 2cm (¾in) square cutter. Attach to the top of the cushion in two lines of alternate colours and add marks around the outside edges of each square with the stitchmark tool no.12 (**A**).

The wool and knitting needles

THE KNITTING NEEDLES

1. **To create the two halves of the knitting needle** held by the cat, you will need 3g (⅛oz) of yellow sugarpaste rolled out to measure 4 x 2cm (1½ x ¾in) and cut into two. Run a line of edible glue down the centre of the strip and place a length of dry spaghetti through the centre (**B**). Fold over the sugarpaste and using tool no.4, trim close to the spaghetti. Roll the piece on the work surface to thin the paste down as much as possible, leaving some spaghetti showing at opposite ends to push into the cat's cheek. From 1g (⅛oz) of black sugarpaste, roll a knob and add to the other end. Set the two halves of the needle aside.

2. **Make a full-length knitting needle** as in Step 1, using a further 2g (⅛oz) of yellow sugarpaste. When complete, push into the ball of wool and set aside.

3. **For the square of knitting** roll out 2g (⅛oz) of dark blue sugarpaste to measure 2cm (¾in) square. Using stitchmark tool no.12, mark lines across the square. Roll some tiny laces to go over the top of the needle, attach the knitting to them (**B**) and set aside.

THE WOOL

For the wool roll 4g (⅛oz) of dark blue sugarpaste into a ball. To make the strands of wool, soften 12g (⅜oz) of dark blue sugarpaste with white vegetable fat (shortening) and fill the cup of a sugar press (or garlic press). Extrude the strands of wool and attach over the ball in a crisscross fashion to cover (**B**). Push one of the knitting needles into the top of the ball and set aside.

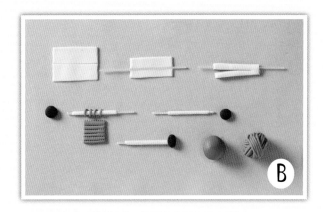

TIP *Because you are softening the paste with white vegetable fat, you will find the sugar press easy to keep clean.*

The cat

THE BODY

1. **To complete the cat** you will need 95g (3⅜oz) of light grey sugarpaste with CMC (Tylose) added. For the body, take off 47g (1⅝oz) and roll into a tall cone shape (**C**). Place the cone on top of the cushion then push a piece of dry spaghetti down through the centre, leaving 2cm (¾in) showing at the top.

2. **Make the back legs** using 12g (⅜oz) of light grey sugarpaste, equally divided. Roll each piece into a ball then lengthen half of the paste to form the lower legs and paws (**C**).

3. **For the front legs** roll 6g (⅛oz) of light grey sugarpaste into a sausage shape and turn up the paws at each end. Cut the piece in half so that each leg measures 4cm (1½in) long. Make a diagonal cut at the top of each leg, turn them on their sides and using tool no.4, remove the bulk from the back by making a diagonal cut (**C**). Attach the legs to the front of the body and indent the paws with the rounded end of tool no.4. Set the leftover paste aside.

4. **To make the tail** you will need 12g (⅜oz) of pale grey sugarpaste, rolled into a fat tapered cone shape (**C**). Make a diagonal cut at the thickest end and attach this to the back of the cat in an upright position.

5. **For the chest fur** take 4g (⅛oz) of white sugarpaste and roll into a flattened cone shape (**C**). Using the rounded end of tool no.4, feather with vertical lines to resemble fur and attach to the front of the body.

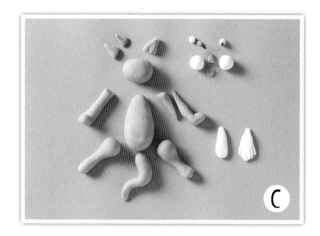

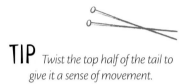

TIP *Twist the top half of the tail to give it a sense of movement.*

THE HEAD

1. **To make the head** roll 18g (⅜oz) of pale grey sugarpaste into a ball then make it slightly oval in shape (**C**). Push a short piece of dry spaghetti into the centre of the face.

2. **To make the cheeks** equally divide 2g (⅛oz) of white sugarpaste and roll each piece into a ball (**C**). Attach to either side of the spaghetti in the centre of the face.

3. **For the nose** make a very small cone shape from 1g (⅛oz) of pink sugarpaste and attach between the two cheeks (**C**).

4. **For the lower lip** take a tiny amount of leftover grey sugarpaste and make a flattened cone shape (**C**). Attach centrally underneath the cheeks and set the leftover paste aside.

5. **For the eyes** take off enough from 1g (⅛oz) of white sugarpaste to make two small eyeballs and attach just above and on either side of the nose. Take off enough from 1g (⅛oz) of dark green sugarpaste to make two smaller balls for the irises. Take off the smallest amount from 1g (⅛oz) of black sugarpaste to make two tiny balls for the pupils, placing them in the centre of the green irises (**C**).

6. **Make the eyelids** by taking off enough from the leftover grey sugarpaste to make two small banana shapes and attaching them over the top of the eyes.

7. **For the ears** make two small cone shapes from the remaining leftover paste and slightly flatten with your fingers. Using the leftover pink sugarpaste, make two smaller cone shapes to line the centre of each ear (**C**). Make a straight cut at the base of each ear and attach to the sides of the head.

8. Push the knitting needles into each side of the cheeks, so that the knitting hangs down on the right side. Place the ball of wool with the knitting needle in front of the cushion and using 1g (⅛oz) of dark blue sugarpaste, roll a thin lace to hang from the end of the knitting, over the cushion and under the ball of wool.

Seamus's Pot of Gold

With the luck of the Irish, Seamus has found his pot of gold on a shamrock at the rainbow's end and he's now ready to take part in all the St. Patrick's Day celebrations! This great traditional character will appeal to many patriotic countrymen.

You will need:

Sugarpaste

- 296g (10½oz) green
- 30g (1⅛oz) flesh
- 29g (1⅛oz) teddy bear brown
- 24g (1oz) yellow
- 21g (¾oz) orange
- 20g (¾oz) black
- 1g (⅛oz) pink

Materials

- 27g (1⅛oz) white modelling paste
- CMC (Tylose)
- White vegetable fat (shortening)
- Sugarflair paste food colour in spruce green, dark brown and white
- Rainbow dust edible metallic gold paint
- Rainbow dust edible dust food colour in pink and dark green
- White paste food colour or edible paint
- Confectioners' glaze
- Edible glue

Equipment

- 12mm (½in), 4cm (2¾in), 8cm (3¼in) circle cutters
- 5mm (¼in), 7mm (⅜in) heart-shaped cutters
- 6mm (¼in), 1cm (⅜in), 2cm (¾in) square cutters
- Cocktail stick (toothpick)
- Basic tool kit (see Modelling Cake Toppers)

The shamrock base

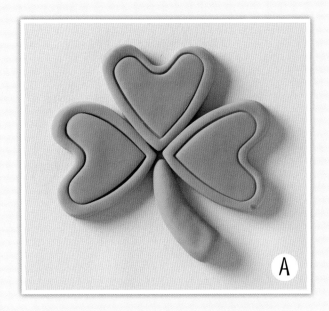

1. **To complete the shamrock base** you will need 140g (5oz) of green sugarpaste rolled out to a 6mm (¼in) thickness. Using a 7mm (⅜in) heart-shaped cutter, take out three hearts to form the shamrock. Indent the hearts by placing a smaller 5mm (¼in) heart-shaped cutter on top of each shape. Position the large hearts onto a card and secure them together where the points meet (**A**).

2. **Make the stem** using a further 10g (¼oz) of the leftover green sugarpaste rolled into a tapered cone shape measuring 6cm (¼in) in length. Flatten slightly with your finger and shape the base of the stem diagonally (**A**). Attach the pointed end to the centre of the shamrock. To highlight the edges of the shamrock, dust around them with dark green edible dust food colour.

Seamus the leprechaun

THE BODY, LEGS AND SHOES

1. **To make the body** you will need 45g (1⅜oz) of green sugarpaste with CMC (Tylose) added. Roll the paste into a tall cone shape measuring 7cm (2¾in) in height (**B**). Push a short piece of dry spaghetti into the hips and place the cone onto a card.

TIP *When using a card to make your models, dust the card first with icing (confectioners') sugar so that the sugarpaste will be easy to remove when complete.*

2. **For the upper legs** you will need 36g (1¼oz) of green sugarpaste rolled into a sausage shape measuring 12cm (4¼in) in length. Make a diagonal cut in the centre and a straight cut at each end. Indent the back of the knees with your finger, about 2cm (¾in) from the end of the legs then bend them (**B**). Push a short piece of dry spaghetti into the end of each leg.

3. **To complete the socks** you will need 24g (1oz) of white modelling paste rolled into a sausage shape measuring 8cm (3¼in) in length. Make a straight cut in the centre then narrow the ankles slightly by rolling on the work surface with your finger (**B**). Push a short piece of dry spaghetti into the end of each sock then slip them over the spaghetti at the ends of the upper legs.

4. **Attach the completed legs** to the hips, keeping the knees bent and supporting the knees from underneath until dry. Make a band to go over the end of each trouser leg using 2g (⅛oz) of green sugarpaste rolled out and cut into two 0.5 x 5cm (¼ x 2in) strips. Secure the strips over the joins between the legs and the socks and add a small ball of green sugarpaste on the side to finish (**B**).

5. **To make the shoes** you will need 13g (⅜oz) of black sugarpaste with CMC added. Take off 12g (⅜oz) and equally divide, then roll each piece into a tapered cone shape. Use a paintbrush handle to mark a line under each shoe, indenting the heels. Slip the shoes over the spaghetti at the end of each sock. Roll out and cut two 12mm (½in) squares from the remaining 1g (⅛oz) of black sugarpaste (**B**) and attach to the top of each shoe.

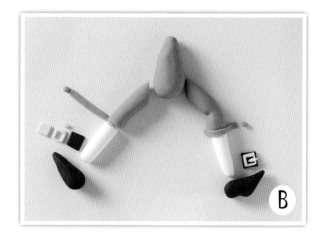

6. **For the buckles** roll out 1g (⅛oz) of yellow sugarpaste and use a cutter to take out two 1cm (⅜in) squares. Take out the centres using a 6mm (¼in) square cutter. Place the buckles onto the top of the shoes then roll two tiny tapered cone shapes with the remaining yellow sugarpaste for the fastenings and place at the centre of each buckle (**B**).

SEAMUS'S CLOTHING

1. **For the shirt** you will need 2g (⅛oz) of white modelling paste, rolled out and cut into a strip measuring 5 x 2.5cm (2 x 1in) (**C**). Attach to the front of the body.

2. **To make the belt** roll out 2g (⅛oz) of black sugarpaste and cut a 0.5 x 4cm (¼ x 2¾in) strip to position on the front of the body. Make a small 1cm (⅜in) square buckle with 1g (⅛oz) of yellow sugarpaste (as described in Step 6 for The body, legs and shoes) and attach to the centre of the belt (**C**).

3. **To complete the waistcoat** you will need 2g (⅛oz) of green sugarpaste, rolled out to measure 2 x 1cm (¾ x ⅜in). Make a diagonal cut at the bottom and a further diagonal cut at the side, tapering off the shape (**C**).

4. **For the necktie** thinly roll out 2g (⅛oz) of yellow sugarpaste and use a cutter to take out a 2cm (¾in) square. Divide the shape into two and make a diagonal cut from the centre to the side on each piece. Make a further diagonal line to the top of each side to shape the ties (**C**) and attach to the top of the body.

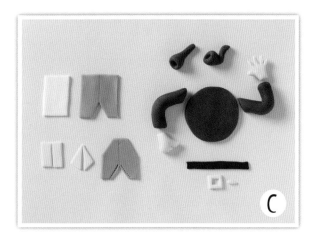

5. **To complete the jacket** you will need 48g (1⅝oz) of green sugarpaste, with spruce green paste food colour added to darken the shade. Take off 30g (1⅛oz) and roll out to a 3mm (⅛in) thickness then take out a circle with an 8cm (3¼in) circle cutter (**C**). Apply some glue around the back and sides of the body then place the circle on the back of the body, bringing the edges around to the front and turning over the collar at the top. The jacket should remain open to show the waistcoat and belt. Push a short piece of dry spaghetti into the shoulders.

TIP *To darken sugarpaste, add paste food colour to a similar shade rather than to white paste, otherwise you will have to use so much paste food colour that the sugarpaste will become too soft to work with.*

6. **Make sleeves** using the remaining darkened green sugarpaste with CMC added, rolled into a 13cm (5⅛in) long sausage shape. Make a straight cut in the centre and bend at each elbow, ensuring that the rounded ends are at the top of the sleeves (**C**).

7. Slip the sleeves over the spaghetti at the shoulders, bringing the right arm to rest on the knee. The left arm is very bent and you will need to insert a long piece of dry spaghetti into the end of the arm, down through the elbow and into the side of the body for support. Push a short piece of dry spaghetti into each wrist to take the hands.

THE HANDS

1. **To make the hands** you will need 4g (⅛oz) of flesh sugarpaste, equally divided. Roll each piece into a fat cone shape and flatten a little with your finger.

2. **For the right hand** mark out the thumb, divide the rest of the palm into four straight fingers using tool no.4 (**C**) and smooth the edges with your fingers.

3. **For the left hand** indent the knuckles and turn the thumb upwards (**C**). Make a straight cut at each wrist and slip the hands over the spaghetti at the end of each sleeve, with the palm of the right hand facing upwards.

THE PIPE

1. **To make the pipe** you will need to darken the sugarpaste by adding some dark brown paste food colour to 3g (⅛oz) of teddy bear brown sugarpaste. Take off 2g (⅛oz) of the darkened sugarpaste, add some CMC and set 1g (⅛oz) aside.

2. Roll the sugarpaste into a ball and narrow half of it with your finger. Push the pointed end of tool no.3 into the rounded end to hollow it out into the bowl and bend the pipe into shape (**C**). Apply some glue to the palm of the left hand and place the pipe into it, bringing the fingers around the bowl.

THE HEAD

1. **To make the head** you will need 25g (1oz) of flesh sugarpaste with CMC added. Take off 24g (1oz) and roll into a ball. Pull down the neck from underneath the ball and gently twist it to lengthen, making a straight cut at the end. Indent the eye area with your finger and shape the face to round off the edges (**D**). Place the head into a flower former to keep it upright and rounded.

2. **For the nose** make a small cone shape from the leftover flesh sugarpaste and attach to the centre of the face, pinching it gently at the end to shape (**D**). Mark the nostrils with the pokey tool no.5.

3. **For the mouth** mark a smile with tool no.11 then open it with the soft end of a paintbrush. Take off a very small amount from 1g (⅛oz) of white modelling paste and roll a banana shape for the teeth. Attach to the top of the mouth and set the leftover modelling paste aside. Keeping the mouth open, take off a tiny amount from 1g (⅛oz) of pink sugarpaste and roll an oval shape for the tongue. Flatten the shape and attach it inside the mouth (**D**).

TIP *It is useful to attach very small parts with the end of your paintbrush, as it allows you to get them into small spaces.*

4. **To make the eyes** roll two small balls from the leftover white modelling paste and position in place, flattening them a little with your finger. Take off enough from 1g (⅛oz) of the leftover dark brown sugarpaste to make two small balls for the irises and press them on top of the eyeballs. To outline the eyes, take a tiny amount from 1g (⅛oz) of black

sugarpaste, roll it on the work surface until it is very thin and use the soft end of your paintbrush to position an outline in place. Highlight the eyes with a cocktail stick (toothpick) dipped into some white paste food colour or edible paint.

5. **For the eyebrows** take off a tiny amount from 1g (⅛oz) of orange sugarpaste to make two tiny tapered curved shapes and position in place using the end of your paintbrush (**D**).

6. **To make the beard and hair** you will need 20g (¾oz) of orange sugarpaste softened with white vegetable fat (shortening). Fill the cup of the sugar press (or garlic press), extrude very short hairs and cut off with tool no.4. Apply some edible glue around the face and add hair all around until complete (**D**).

7. **To make the ears** take off enough from 1g (⅛oz) of flesh sugarpaste to make two oval shapes. Flatten them with your fingers and indent the sides of the ears with a paintbrush. Attach to the sides of the head and indent the base of each ear with the end of a paintbrush (**D**).

8. Dust the cheeks with a soft brush and some pink dust food colour and apply confectioners' glaze to the shoes and eyes to make them shine.

9. Apply some edible glue around the top of the body and back of the collar and slip the head in an upright position over the spaghetti at the top.

THE HAT

1. **To complete the hat** you will need 22g (⅞oz) of green sugarpaste. Roll out 10g (¼oz) and cut out a circle for the brim with a 4cm (1¾in) circle cutter. Roll the remaining green sugarpaste into a ball then into a fat cone shape for the top of the hat and flatten the top and base of the cone (**D**). Apply some edible glue to the brim and attach to the head, shaping the brim. Push a piece of dry spaghetti into the top of the head, leaving 2cm (¾in) showing. Slip the top of the hat over the spaghetti to secure.

2. **Make a band** to go around the hat using 3g (⅛oz) of black sugarpaste rolled out to measure 0.5 x 8cm (¼ x 3¼in). Apply a line of edible glue around the hat and attach the band.

3. **Add a shamrock** using 1g (⅛oz) of green sugarpaste, taking out three shapes with a 6mm (¼in) heart-shaped cutter. Mark a line down the centre of each heart with tool no.4 (**D**) and arrange on the band.

The pot of gold

1. **To complete the pot** you will need 26g (1oz) of teddy bear brown sugarpaste with CMC added. Take off 25g (1oz), roll into a smooth ball then hollow out the top a little with your fingers and shape the pot (**E**).

2. **Make the lugs for the sides** using the remaining 1g (⅛oz) of teddy bear brown sugarpaste, rolled into two small sausage shapes. Use the handle of a paintbrush to narrow the shapes in the centre and flatten each end with your finger (**E**). Push a short piece of dry spaghetti into each side of the pot and slip the lugs over the top.

3. **For the coins** roll out 20g (¾oz) of yellow sugarpaste and take out thirteen circles using a 12mm (½in) circle cutter (**E**). Apply some glue to the pot and arrange eleven coins over the top. Place the pot of gold on the right hand side of the leprechaun and attach the remaining two coins to the shamrock leaf.

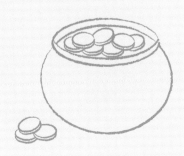

TIP *For a sparkling finishing touch, paint the coins with edible metallic gold paint.*

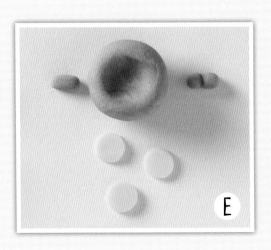

E

Panda Playtime

This playful family scene features a carefree mummy panda enjoying a bit of rough and tumble with her mischievous little boy, while her baby happily plays peek-a-boo in a bowl of rice. They are all having the time of their lives!

You will need:

Sugarpaste

- 70g (2½oz) black
- 5g (⅛oz) green
- 4g (⅛oz) teddy bear brown
- 1g (⅛oz) atlantic blue (dark)
- 1g (⅛oz) pink

Materials

- 188g (6¼oz) white modelling paste
- CMC (Tylose)
- White paste food colour
- Edible glue

Equipment

- Cocktail stick (toothpick)
- Basic tool kit (see Modelling Cake Toppers)

The mummy panda

THE BODY, LEGS AND ARMS

1. **To complete the body** you will need 75g (3oz) of white modelling paste, rolled into a fat cone shape and placed down onto card.

2. **For the black band of fur** roll out 6g (⅛oz) of black sugarpaste into a sausage shape and widen to a measurement of 2 x 6cm (⅜ x 2½in) with your rolling pin (**A**). Divide the shape equally in half and attach the rounded ends at the centre of the chest, smoothing the remaining paste into the side of the body.

TIP *You do not need to continue the black band around the back of the body, as it will not be seen.*

3. **To make the legs** you will need 22g (⅞oz) of black sugarpaste with CMC (Tylose) added. Roll into an even sausage shape and turn up the rounded ends to form the feet. Lift up the end of the sugarpaste and use your index finger to push the sugarpaste towards the length of the leg, flattening the bottom of the feet. Equally divide the shape with a straight cut in the centre (**A**).

4. Push a piece of dry spaghetti into down through each leg to give it support, leaving 2cm (¾in) showing at the top. Push the spaghetti into the body, supporting the left foot so that it is higher than the right foot until dry.

5. **To make the pads for the feet and paws** you will need 3g (⅛oz) of teddy bear brown sugarpaste. Take off 2g (⅛oz) and divide equally to make the pads for the feet. Take off two thirds and roll into a ball for the pad, flatten with your finger and secure to the base of the foot. From the remaining paste, roll three small round balls and arrange around the top of the large pad. Set the leftover paste aside.

6. **To complete the arms** you will need 20g (¾oz) of black sugarpaste with CMC added. Roll into a sausage shape and make a diagonal cut in the centre. Push a piece of spaghetti into each arm for support, leaving 1cm (⅜in) showing at the diagonal cut. Secure the arms, pushing the spaghetti into the body so that they will stay upright. Using the leftover teddy bear brown sugarpaste, roll two small balls and press onto the inside of the paws for the pads (**A**).

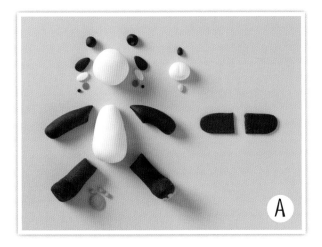

THE HEAD

1. **To make the head** you will need 44g (1⅝oz) of white modelling paste. Take off 39g (1½oz) and roll into a ball (**A**). Push a piece of dry spaghetti into the top of the cone, and slip the head over the top.

TIP *The head is slightly lifted up and turned to one side and will therefore require some support until dry.*

2. **For the muzzle** roll the remaining 5g (⅛oz) of white modelling paste into a ball and place on the front of the head. Mark a line down the centre with tool no.4 and use the smiley tool no.5 to mark a mouth at the base of the line. Use the pokey tool no.5 to make a hole for the nose at the top of the line. Use the soft end of a paintbrush to open the mouth. Take off enough from 1g (⅛oz) of pink sugarpaste to make a small oval shape for the tongue (**A**), secure inside the mouth and set the rest of the sugarpaste aside.

3. **To make the eyes** you will need 1g (⅛oz) of black sugarpaste. Take off enough to make two black oval shapes and place at an angle, just above and on either side of the muzzle. From 1g (⅛oz) of white modelling paste roll two smaller oval shapes for the eyes, then attach over the top of the black ovals. Make the blue irises by taking off enough from 1g (⅛oz) of atlantic blue (dark) sugarpaste to roll two small round balls, setting the remainder aside. Place these over the white shapes and finally add two tiny black sugarpaste balls for the pupils (**A**).

4. **To make the ears** you will need 1g (⅛oz) of black sugarpaste equally divided and each piece rolled into a ball (**A**). Position the ears on each side of the head and press into place with end of tool no.1.

The little boy panda

THE BODY, LEGS AND ARMS

1. **For the body** you will need 12g (⅜oz) of white modelling paste rolled into a cone shape (**B**). Push a piece of dry spaghetti down through the centre, leaving 1cm (⅜in) showing at the top. Place the body upright on a card to complete the figure.

2. **To make the legs** you will need to roll 8g (¼oz) of black sugarpaste with CMC added into a 6cm (2½in) long sausage shape. Turn up the feet at the rounded ends and make a straight cut in the centre to divide (**B**). Push a short piece of dry spaghetti into the sides of the cone shape and slip the legs over the top.

3. **For the black fur bands** you will need 2g (⅛oz) of black sugarpaste with CMC added, equally divided. Roll each piece into an rectangular shape and flatten a little with a rolling pin to widen. Place the ends of the bands together at the back of the panda and bring to the front (**B**).

4. **To complete the arms** you will need to roll 5g (⅛oz) of black sugarpaste with CMC added into a 6cm (2½in) long sausage shape then make a diagonal cut in the centre (**B**). To keep the arms outstretched, push a length of dry spaghetti down through each arm, leaving 1cm (⅜in) showing at the top to push into the shoulders.

5. Place the body on to the top of the mummy panda and secure with edible glue. Position the legs as you desire before they dry out.

(B)

THE HEAD

1. **To make the head** roll 7g (¼oz) of white modelling paste into a ball (**B**) and slip over the top of the spaghetti at the neck.

2. **For the muzzle** roll 2g (⅛oz) of white modelling paste into a ball and place onto the front of the head. Mark a line down the centre of the muzzle and use tool no.11 to mark a smile at the base of the line, opening the mouth with the soft end of a paintbrush (**B**). Roll a small oval shape from the leftover pink sugarpaste for the tongue and insert it inside the mouth. Using the pokey tool no.5, mark a hole at the top of the line for the nose then roll a tiny oval shape with black sugarpaste and secure it inside the hole.

3. **Make the eyes and ears** (**B**) following Steps 3 and 4 for The mummy panda and position in place.

The baby panda and rice bowl

THE RICE BOWL

1. **To complete the bowl** you will need 20g (¾oz) of white modelling paste, rolled into a ball and placed on the end of a rolling pin. Hollow out the bowl and work it down the pin with your fingers to make a smooth shape (**C**). Remove from the rolling pin and level the edges with tool no.4 if necessary. The completed bowl should be 2cm (¾in) in height.

2. **For the chopsticks** you will need to make a cream shade by adding 5g (⅛oz) of white modelling paste to 1g (⅛oz) of teddy bear brown sugarpaste. Roll out to measure 1 x 6cm (⅜ x 2½in) then run a line of edible glue down the centre and press a piece of dry spaghetti into it. Fold over the sugarpaste and trim off the excess with tool no.4 (**D**). Roll the chopsticks on the work surface to thin as much as possible. You will need two chopsticks measuring 5cm (2in) in length.

3. **To complete the bamboo decoration** you will need 5g (¼oz) of green sugarpaste with CMC added. Take off enough to roll two thin stems then mark them diagonally across with tool no.4 (**C**) and secure them to the side of the rice bowl.

4. **Make the leaves** with the remaining green sugarpaste, taking off small amounts and rolling them into sausage shapes with pointed ends. Mark down the centre of each leaf with tool no.4 (**C**). Make eight leaves and attach them to the bamboo stems to complete.

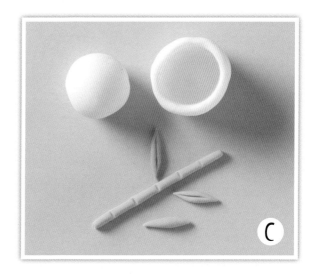

THE BABY PANDA

1. **To make the body** form a small cone shape with 10g (¼oz) of white modelling paste (**D**). Push a length of dry spaghetti down through the centre, leaving 1cm (⅜in) showing at the top. Place inside the rice bowl.

2. To make the front paws, roll 3g (⅛oz) of black sugarpaste with CMC added into a small sausage shape. Make a diagonal cut in the centre (**D**) and attach to the top of the cone and over the sides of the bowl.

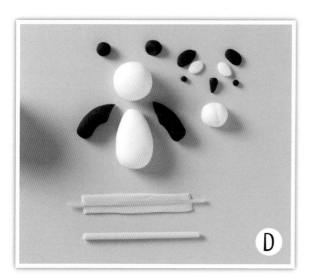

3. **To complete the head** you will need 7g (¼oz) of white modelling paste rolled into a ball and an additional 1g (⅛oz) for the muzzle (**D**). Mark a line down the centre of the muzzle, a hole for the mouth with the pokey tool no.5 and a further hole at the top of the line for the nose.

4. **For the black details** you will need 2g (⅛oz) of black sugarpaste with CMC added. Make the eyes and ears (**D**) following Steps 3 and 4 for The mummy panda, this time using black sugarpaste for the irises, omitting the pupils and highlighting the eyes with a cocktail stick (toothpick) dipped into some white paste food colour. Roll a small black cone for the nose and place this inside the hole to complete. Cross the chopsticks over at the back of the bowl.

Come Fly With Me

An adventurous seagull is hitching a ride with this cheerful pilot. Chocks away, hold on tight and up and away they go, into the sunset for a daring adventure! Aeroplane enthusiasts young or old will just love this comical centrepiece.

You will need:

Sugarpaste

- 126g (4½oz) red
- 9g (¼oz) flesh
- 8g (¼oz) dark brown
- 7g (¼oz) grey
- 2g (⅛oz) yellow
- 2g (⅛oz) light brown
- 2g (⅛oz) pale blue
- 2g (⅛oz) orange

Materials

- 4g (⅛oz) white modelling paste
- Confectioners' glaze
- CMC (Tylose)
- Rainbow Dust edible metallic silver paint
- Rainbow Dust pink dust food colour
- Sugarflair black liquid food colour
- Edible glue

Equipment

- 8mm (⅜in) star cutter
- 6mm (¼in), 3cm (1¼in) circle cutters
- Paintbrush no.0000
- Basic tool kit (see Modelling Cake Toppers)

The aeroplane

MAIN BODY AND COCKPIT

1. **To make the main body** of the plane you will need 100g (4oz) of red sugarpaste with CMC (Tylose) added. Roll the sugarpaste into a fat carrot shape, taper the end with your fingers and place onto a dusted card. Turn the tail of the plane upward (**A**) and support the underneath of it with a wedge-shaped sponge to keep its shape until dry. Also support the front end of the plane to keep it off the card. Push a piece of dry spaghetti into the nose of the plane, leaving 3cm (1¼in) showing to support the cone and propellers.

2. **To form the cockpit** push the end of a rolling pin into the top of the plane to hollow it out. Smooth around the edges with your fingers and lift up the front to form the windscreen (**A**).

TIP *If you do not have shaped foam for your supports, shape some sugarpaste and wrap it in clingfilm – it will do the job perfectly.*

THE TAIL FINS AND WINGS

1. **To make the tail fins** you will need 4g (⅛oz) of red sugarpaste with CMC added, rolled into a flattened sausage shape. Taper the ends and divide equally then trim the length of each piece to 2cm (¾in) in length (**A**). Push a length of dry spaghetti through each piece and into the side of the tail, securing with edible glue.

2. **For the wings** you will need 16g (½oz) of red sugarpaste with CMC added. Roll into a flattened sausage shape, keeping the ends rounded and make a straight cut in the centre. Trim each piece to measure 2 x 4cm (¾ x 1½in) (**A**). Push two lengths of dry spaghetti into the straight edges of the wings then push into each side of the plane. Support each wing from underneath until dry and firm.

THE ENGINE COVER AND PROPELLER

1. **To make the circular engine cover** you will need 6g (⅛oz) of yellow sugarpaste with CMC added. Roll out to a 5mm (¼in) thickness and cut into a strip to measure 1.2 x 9cm (½ x 3½in). Make a straight cut at each end (**A**) and glue together to form a circle then attach to the front of the plane.

2. **For the propeller base** roll 4g (⅛oz) of grey sugarpaste with CMC added into a fat cone shape and flatten the widest end (**A**). Slip over the spaghetti at the front of the plane.

3. **To make the propellers** you will need 3g (⅛oz) of grey sugarpaste with CMC added rolled into a sausage shape measuring 4cm (1¾in) in length. Narrow the shape in the centre and work each end to widen and flatten into the propeller shape. Mark the centre of the propeller with a 6mm (¼in) circle cutter (**A**) then slip over the spaghetti showing at the end of the cone. Paint the propellers with edible metallic silver paint.

4. **Decorate the outline of the cockpit** and the side of the plane by rolling 1g (⅛oz) of yellow sugarpaste into a fine lace and attaching as shown with edible glue. Using a 8mm (⅜in) star cutter, take out two shapes (**A**) and secure them to the tail of the plane.

The pilot

THE BODY, ARMS AND HANDS

1. **To make the body** roll 3g (⅛oz) of dark brown sugarpaste into a cone shape (**B**) and mould the shape so that it sits inside the plane. Push a piece of dry spaghetti down through the centre, leaving 3cm (1¼in) showing.

2. **To make the arms** roll 1g (⅛oz) of dark brown sugarpaste into a sausage shape and make a diagonal cut in the centre (**B**). Attach the left arm to the top of the body, placing the rest inside the cockpit (no hand is required for the left arm). Bend the right arm and attach to the shoulder, resting the elbow on the side of the cockpit. Push a piece of dry spaghetti down from the wrist to the elbow to keep it in a bent upright position, allowing 1cm (⅜in) of spaghetti to show at the end to take the hand.

3. **To create the hand** roll 1g (⅛oz) of flesh sugarpaste into a flattened cone shape. Mark out the thumb with tool no.4, cut out the index finger and roll to remove the edges. Fold the rest of the fingers into the palm of the hand and mark the fingers with tool no.4 (**B**). Make a straight cut at the wrist, and slip the hand over the spaghetti at the end of the arm. The palm of the hand should face upwards.

4. **To make the necktie** roll out 2g (⅛oz) of pale blue sugarpaste and use tool no. 4 to cut out a triangular shape measuring 3cm (1¼in) across (**B**). Fold over the top to make a soft fold and attach loosely around the pilot's neck, with the points meeting at the back.

THE HEAD

1. **To form the head** roll 7g (¼oz) of flesh sugarpaste into a ball and pull down the neck from underneath. Shape the chin with the side of your finger as you roll the neck, pulling it downward to lengthen (**B**). Dust the cheeks with a soft brush and some pink dust food colour.

2. **Make a large nose** by taking off enough from 1g (⅛oz) of flesh sugarpaste to form a cone shape (**B**). Attach to the centre of the face and mark the nostrils with tool no.5.

3. **Mark a smile** with tool no.11 and open the mouth with the soft end of a paintbrush. Take off a tiny amount from 1g (⅛oz) of white modelling paste and roll into a banana shape for the teeth. Curve the shape and insert into the top of the mouth (**B**).

4. **To make the moustache** take off a small amount from 1g (⅛oz) of light brown sugarpaste and roll two tapered cone shapes. Attach them directly under the nose, turning up at the ends (**B**).

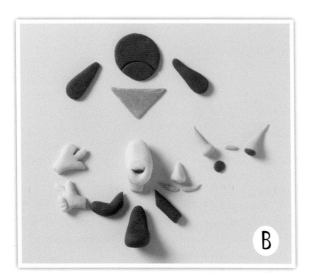

B

TIP *The pilot does not need ears or eyes as they are covered with other items.*

THE GOGGLES AND HAT

1. **To make the goggles** equally divide 1g (⅛oz) of light brown sugarpaste, roll each piece into a short fat cone shape and flatten the widest ends (**B**). Taper the other ends so that they fit around the side of the head.

2. **For the lenses** roll out 1g (⅛oz) of dark brown sugarpaste, take out two circles with a 6mm (¼in) circle cutter and attach over the flat end of the goggles. Position in place leaving a small gap in the centre and bring the tapered ends around the sides of the head. Roll a thin lace for the bridge (**B**) and paint the lenses with confectioners' glaze.

3. **To complete the hat** you will need 3g (⅛oz) of black sugarpaste. Take off 2g (⅛oz) and roll out. Take out a 3cm (1¼in) circle with a cutter and mark the back of the cap with the edge of the cutter. Apply some edible glue around the pilot's head and fit the hat. Equally divide the remaining paste and roll each piece into a tapered cone shape. Flatten the shapes with your finger (**B**) and attach to the sides of the head.

The seagull

1. **To make the body** roll 3g (⅛oz) of white modelling paste into a ball then pull out the tail and a thin neck (**C**). Push a piece of dry spaghetti down through the neck, leaving 1cm (⅜in) showing at the top to take the head.

2. **Make the feet** by taking off enough from 1g (⅛oz) of orange sugarpaste with CMC added to make two small tapered cone shapes (**C**). Flatten the ends and turn up the feet with your finger. Cut out two 'V' shapes with tool no.4 for the claws. Push a length of dry spaghetti down each leg and into the feet then push the ends into the body.

3. **To make the wings** equally divide 1g (⅛oz) of white modelling paste. Roll into two cones, flattening one edge and shaping into a curve. Using tool no.4, mark three diagonal lines down the edges for feathers (**C**). Push a short piece of dry spaghetti into each side and slip the wings over, pressing them firmly to the body. Edge the wings and tail with black liquid food colour, using a fine brush for the feathers.

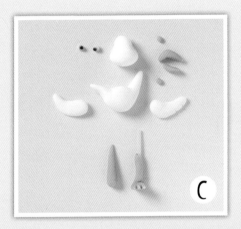

4. **To make the head** you will need to roll 1g (⅛oz) of white modelling paste into a small cone shape. Pinch out the cheeks with your fingers to widen (**C**). Push a short piece of dry spaghetti into the centre to support the beak.

5. **To make the beak** you will need 1g (⅛oz) of orange sugarpaste, divided into two, with a larger amount for the top of the beak. Make a flattened, slightly bent cone shape for the top of the beak, slip over the spaghetti on the face and secure with edible glue. For the smaller, lower part, roll slightly less orange sugarpaste into a flattened cone shape. Join the backs of the beaks together, keeping the front open and marking two air holes at the top with the end of tool no.4. Roll two small balls from orange sugarpaste and attach to either side of the beak (**C**).

6. **For the eyes** roll two very small balls from 1g (⅛oz) of yellow sugarpaste (**C**) and attach them very close together above the beak. Paint on the eyebrows and add a small black dot for the pupils using black liquid food colour.

7. **Add three hairs** to the top of the head by rolling three tiny tapered cone shapes from 1g (⅛oz) of white modelling paste. Secure the bird to the tail of the plane.

Double Trouble

Playful twins, Amy and Harry, look so innocent and peaceful sitting with their toys, but who knows how much trouble they are scheming for later? This simple design would make an adorable cake topper for a christening, first birthday or baby shower.

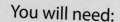

You will need:

Sugarpaste
- 80g (2⅞oz) pale pink
- 39g (1½oz) flesh
- 7g (¼oz) fuchsia pink
- 3g (⅛oz) lime green
- 3g (⅛oz) yellow
- 3g (⅛oz) pale yellow
- 2g (⅛oz) orange
- 1g (⅛oz) atlantic blue (dark)
- 1g (⅛oz) lincoln green
- 1g (⅛oz) dark brown
- 1g (⅛oz) teddy bear brown

Materials
- 10g (¼oz) white modelling paste
- CMC (Tylose)
- Edible glue

Equipment
- 6mm (¼in), 1cm (⅜in), 2cm (¾in) circle cutters
- Basic tool kit (see Modelling Cake Toppers)

Baby Amy

AMY'S BODY

1. **To complete Baby Amy** you will need 79g (2⅞oz) of pale pink sugarpaste with CMC (Tylose) added. Take off 40g (1½oz) for the body and roll into a cone shape (**A**). Push a piece of dry spaghetti down through the centre, leaving 2cm (¾in) showing at the top.

2. **For the legs** take off a further 24g (1oz) and roll into a sausage shape measuring 10cm (4in) in length. Turn up the ends with your finger to form the feet, make a straight cut in the centre then make a diagonal cut at the top of each leg to attach to the body. Keep the legs spread apart (**A**).

3. **Make the arms** with the remaining 15g (½oz) of pink sugarpaste rolled into a sausage shape measuring 8cm (3¼in) in length. Make a straight cut in the centre, bending the centre of the right arm for the elbow (**A**). Push a short piece of dry spaghetti into the top of the cone, slip the rounded end of the right arm over the top and rest this arm onto the leg. Attach the left arm to the shoulder and stretch it out to reach the foot. Push a short piece of dry spaghetti into the end of each arm to take the hands.

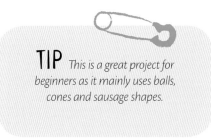

TIP *This is a great project for beginners as it mainly uses balls, cones and sausage shapes.*

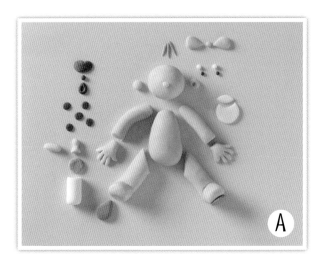

4. **For the soles of the feet** you will need 1g (⅛oz) of fuchsia pink sugarpaste mixed together with 1g (⅛oz) of white modelling paste to make a deeper shape of pink. Equally divide the paste, roll a small, flattened cone shape for each pad (**A**) making one end a little wider than the other and secure to the feet.

5. **To make the hands** you will need 2g (⅛oz) of flesh sugarpaste, equally divided and each piece rolled into a flattened cone shape. Using tool no.4, mark out the thumb and four fingers and round off all the edges (**A**). Make a straight cut at each wrist and slip the hands over the spaghetti. The left hand should be secured to the foot and the palm of the right hand should face the baby.

6. **For the bib** roll out 2g (⅛oz) of white modelling paste and cut out a 2cm (¾in) circle. Using the edge of the cutter, take out a curve at the top (**A**) and attach to the front of the body. Set the leftover paste aside.

7. **For the spots** roll out 6g (¼oz) of fuchsia pink sugarpaste, take out some circles with a 6mm (¼in) circle cutter and attach them randomly over the body, legs and arms (**A**). Set the leftover paste aside.

AMY'S HEAD

1. **To make the head** you will need 17g (⅝oz) of flesh sugarpaste with some CMC added. Take off 16g (½oz) and set the rest of the sugarpaste aside. Roll the paste into a ball then shape it into a slight oval (**A**) and slip the head over the spaghetti at the top of the body.

2. **To make the nose** roll a tiny oval from the leftover flesh sugarpaste (**A**) and attach to the centre of the face.

3. **For the ears** roll the remaining flesh sugarpaste into two balls. Secure to each side of the head in their rounded shape and indent with the end of a paintbrush (**A**).

4. **To make the soother** take off a tiny amount from the leftover fuchsia sugarpaste, roll into an oval shape and flatten with your finger. Indent the top centre of the shape with the end of a paintbrush and secure to the mouth area. Roll a very small lace to form into a circle, attach to the centre of the shape then finish with a tiny central ball (**A**).

5. **To make the eyes** take off a tiny amount from the leftover white modelling paste from the bib and roll two small balls. Position them just above and on either side of the nose. Take off an even smaller amount from 1g (⅛oz) of dark brown sugarpaste for the irises and attach over the tops of the eyes (**A**). Set the remaining dark brown paste aside for Harry.

TIP *Keeping the eyes close together will make the face look extra cute.*

6. **To make the hair** mix together 1g (⅛oz) of white sugarpaste and a small amount taken from 1g (⅛oz) of teddy bear brown sugarpaste to make a light brown shade. Roll three very thin tapered cone shapes and attach to the top of the head (**A**). Set the remaining sugarpaste aside.

7. **To complete the bow** you will need 1g (⅛oz) of pale pink sugarpaste. Take off a small amount and roll into two flattened cone shapes. Place the cones on their sides with their points in the centre and secure to the hair. Add a tiny pink ball and place into the centre of the bow (**A**).

AMY'S BOTTLE

1. **For the bottle** roll 3g (⅛oz) of white modelling paste into a fat sausage shape measuring 2.5cm (1in) in length (**A**).

2. **To make the bottle top** you will need 1g (⅛oz) of pink sugarpaste and 1g (⅛oz) of flesh sugarpaste. Roll out the pink sugarpaste and with a cutter, take out a 1cm (⅜in) circle (**A**) then place this on top of the bottle.

3. **Make the teat** by rolling the flesh sugarpaste into a small sausage shape then indenting the centre of the shape to narrow and widening the base a little. Attach the teat on top of the pink circle and make a small hole in the top using the pokey tool no.5 (**A**).

4. Apply some glue to the palm of Amy's right hand and attach the bottle in an upright position.

Baby Harry

THE BODY AND HEAD

1. **To complete Baby Harry** you will need 79g (2⅞oz) of pale blue sugarpaste with CMC added. Take off 40g (1½oz) for the body and roll into a cone shape (**B**). Place the cone on to the flat surface of a dusted card and push a short piece of dry spaghetti into the hip line.

2. **Make the legs** using 24g (1oz) of pale blue sugarpaste as in Step 2 for Amy's body, this time making a diagonal cut at the tops of the legs. Bend each leg at the knee area (**B**) and slip over the spaghetti on the body. Both legs are in the air, with the right leg leaning forward towards the top of the body and the left leg positioned straight upwards.

3. **For the soles of the feet** you will need 3g (⅛oz) of white sugarpaste mixed together with a tiny amount of atlantic blue sugarpaste (dark) to make a deeper shade of blue. Take off 2g (⅛oz) of the mixed blue paste and equally divide. Shape the pads as in Step 4 for Amy's body then attach to the bottom of the feet (**B**). Set the leftover dark blue sugarpaste aside.

4. **Make the arms** using the remaining 15g (½oz) of pale blue sugarpaste rolled into a sausage shape as in Step 3 for Amy's body, this time making a diagonal cut in the centre for the top of the arms (**B**). Push a short piece of dry spaghetti into the straight ends to take the hands.

5. **Make the hands** using 2g (⅛oz) of flesh sugarpaste, equally divided, following Step 5 for Amy's body. Slip the hands over the spaghetti at the end of each arm. Attach the right arm to the top of the body and secure the hand to the end of the right foot. Secure the left arm to the top of the body and position it so that it is laying flat on the card. Keep the index finger pointed on the left hand and curl the other three fingers towards the palm, keeping the thumb up (**B**).

6. **Make the bib** following Step 6 for Amy's body, using 2g (⅛oz) of white modelling paste (**B**).

7. **Make the head** following Step 1 for Amy's head, using 17g (⅝oz) of flesh sugarpaste. Repeat Steps 2, 3 and 5 for Amy's head to make the eyes, nose, ears and hair. To make the soother, follow Step 4 for Amy's head, using the leftover dark blue sugarpaste (**B**).

HARRY'S RATTLE

1. **To complete the rattle** you will need 3g (⅛oz) of pale yellow sugarpaste. Take off 2g (⅛oz) and roll into a ball then pull out the handle and roll out with your fingers to lengthen. Push a length of dry spaghetti down through the handle and into the ball (**B**).

2. **For the handle** roll out the remaining pale yellow sugarpaste and cut out two 1cm (⅜in) circles. Take out the centres with a 6mm (¼in) circle cutter. Drop a circle over the handle and secure around the ball at the end (**B**). Place the other circle over Harry's thumb and attach the rattle.

The stacking rings

1. **To make the base** roll 3g (⅛oz) of yellow sugarpaste into a ball and flatten with your finger to a width of 2cm (¾in) (**B**).

2. **For the rings** roll 3g (⅛oz) of lime green sugarpaste into a ball, flatten to a width of 18mm (⅝in) and place on top of the yellow base (**B**). Roll 2g (⅛oz) of orange sugarpaste and flatten to a width of 13mm (½in). Finally roll 1g (⅛oz) of lincoln green (dark) sugarpaste and flatten to a width of 1cm (⅜in).

3. **For the pole** push a piece of dry spaghetti down through the centre of the rings, leaving 1cm (⅜in) showing at the top. Make the knob using 1g (⅛oz) of atlantic blue (dark) sugarpaste rolled into an oval shape and secured over the top of the spaghetti.

Jolly Santa

It's that wonderful time of year when children from all over the world eagerly await a gift from Santa. This traditional, Victorian-style figure will not disappoint with his bulging sack full of toys and sweets for boys and girls that have been good all year.

You will need:

Sugarpaste

- 257g (9⅛oz) red
- 125g (4½oz) white
- 107g (3¾oz) amethyst
- 98g (3⅜oz) teddy bear brown
- 36g (1¼oz) flesh
- 30g (1⅛oz) black
- 8g (¼oz) yellow
- 7g (¼oz) green
- Rainbow Dust pink dust food colour
- Sugarflair paste food colour in dark brown, melon and spruce green
- Edible glue

Materials

- 59g (2¼oz) white modelling paste
- CMC (Tylose)
- White vegetable fat (shortening)

Equipment

- 6 x 5cm (2¼ x 2in) polystyrene former
- 6mm (¼in), 12mm (½in) square cutters
- 3cm (1¼in), 7cm (2¾in) circle cutters
- Basic tool kit (see Modelling Cake Toppers)

Santa

THE SEAT

1. **To make the seat** cover a 6 x 5cm (2½ x 2in) polystyrene former with 100g (4oz) of amethyst sugarpaste, rolled to a 5mm (¼in) thickness. Apply some edible glue to the top and sides and place the sugarpaste over the top. Secure the paste around the top first then work your way down to the base, trimming off the edges.

> **TIP** *Secure the top edge firmly before working on the remaining paste to avoid the sugarpaste stretching and breaking.*

THE BOOTS

1. **To make the boots** you will need 28g (1⅛oz) of black sugarpaste with some CMC (Tylose) added, rolled into a sausage shape. Turn up the rounded ends to form the feet and make a straight cut in the centre to form two boots (**A**).

2. **Make soles for the boots** using 4g (⅛oz) of teddy bear brown sugarpaste with CMC added, equally divided. Roll each piece into a small sausage shape, slightly longer than the bottom of each boot, and flatten the front and back with your finger. Attach the soles to the boots and set them aside (**A**).

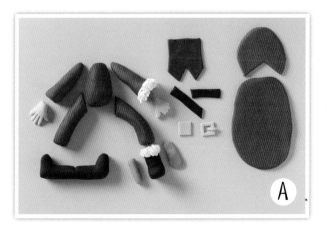

THE BODY, LEGS AND CLOTHING

1. **To complete the body and legs** you will need 112g (3⅞oz) of red sugarpaste with a teaspoon of CMC kneaded in. Take off 66g (2⅜oz), roll into a fat cone shape (**A**) and place in the centre of the stool. Push a piece of dry spaghetti down through the centre, leaving 2cm (¾in) showing at the top.

2. **For the legs** roll the remaining 46g (1⅝oz) of red sugarpaste into a fat sausage shape measuring 14cm (5½in) in length. Make a diagonal cut in the centre and bend each leg at the knee (**A**). Secure the top of the legs to the hips and bring the backs of the knees over the edge of the seat. Push a piece of dry spaghetti into the end of each leg, leaving 2cm (¾in) showing. Push the boots over the spaghetti and connect to the ends of the legs, spreading the feet apart to create space to place the sack between them.

3. **For the fur trims** soften 10g (¼oz) of white sugarpaste with white vegetable fat (shortening) and fill the cup of the sugar press (or garlic press). Extrude very short strands, cut them off with tool no.4 and attach the fur around the bottom of each trouser leg (**A**).

4. **To make the belt** roll out 2g (⅛oz) of black sugarpaste and cut into a 1 x 10cm (⅜ x 4in) strip. Cut off 4cm (2¾in) and glue around the left side of the waistline. Attach the remaining piece on the other side and cross it over at the front to hide the join. Make a buckle using 1g (⅛oz) of the cream sugarpaste cut into a 12mm (½in) square. Take out the centre with a 6mm (¼in) square cutter and attach to the centre of the belt. Roll a tiny oval for the prong and attach in the centre of the buckle (**A**).

5. **For the waistcoat front** add spruce green paste food colour to 5g (⅛oz) of white modelling paste. Roll out, cut a shape measuring 5 x 4cm (2 x 1¾in) and mark a faint line down the centre with tool no.4. Take out a triangular shape at the bottom of the line then make a diagonal cut from each point to the side. The waistcoat should now have two points at the front (**A**). Attach to the front of the body so that the points rest on either side of the buckle.

6. **Make the main body of the coat** in one piece using 67g (2⅜oz) of red sugarpaste. Roll into a sausage shape measuring 12cm (4¾in) in length, widen with a rolling pin to a width of 10cm (4in) and smooth around the edges of the shape with your fingers (**A**). Apply some glue to the back and sides of the body and the back of the seat then wrap the coat around from the back, bringing the edges to the front. Edge the coat with a fur trim using 60g (2¼oz) of softened white sugarpaste (see Step 3).

7. **To complete the sleeves** you will need 30g (1⅛oz) of red sugarpaste with CMC added, equally divided. Roll each piece into a long cone shape, thinning a little at the top (**A**) and make a hole in the end of each sleeve using the pointed end of tool no.3. Apply some edible glue on the inside of the arms and attach to each side of the body, resting on top of each leg. Push a piece of dry spaghetti into the end of the sleeves.

8. **For the collar** you will need 23g (1oz) of red sugarpaste. Cut out a 7cm (2¾in) circle then cut out a triangle shape from the bottom and shape the top of the circle into a dome shape with your fingers (**A**). Place the collar behind the spaghetti at the neck and bring the points forward. Edge the collar with a fur trim using 20g (¾oz) of softened white sugarpaste (see Step 3).

9. **To make the hands** equally divide 8g (¼oz) of flesh sugarpaste and add some CMC. Roll each piece into a cone shape, mark out the thumbs and round off all the edges with your fingers. Indent the knuckles on the left hand with tool no.4 and mark out four fingers on the right hand, rolling them with your fingers until smooth. Make a straight cut at each wrist and attach the hands over the spaghetti at the end of the sleeves, leaving the right hand open (**A**). Edge the sleeves with a fur trim using 10g (¼oz) of softened white sugarpaste (see Step 3).

SANTA'S HEAD

1. **To complete the head** you will need 28g (1⅛oz) of flesh sugarpaste with CMC added. Take off 27g (1oz) and roll into a ball, pulling down the neck from underneath. Shape the eye area with your finger and make a straight cut at the base of the neck (**B**). Place the head into a flower former to complete.

B

6. **To make the beard** soften 25g (1oz) of white sugarpaste with white vegetable fat and fill the cup of the sugar press. Extrude some strands to 3cm (1¼in) in length and arrange in a line. Take a 4cm (2¾in) circle cutter and make a curve in the top of the beard. Apply some glue around the face and secure the beard, adding more strands at the end if necessary so that it tapers off to the temples. Add a row of hair around the back of the head. When the beard is complete, roll a tiny banana shape from the leftover flesh sugarpaste for the lower lip (**B**).

7. **To form the moustache** make two tapered cone shapes from the leftover white paste used for the beard. Attach under the nose, bringing the ends over the top of the beard (**B**). Dust the cheeks with some pink dust food colour, using a clean soft brush.

SANTA'S HAT

1. **To make the hat** you will need 15g (½oz) of red sugarpaste with CMC added. Roll the sugarpaste into a tapered cone shape, open the widest end with your fingers and attach to the top of the head (**B**).

2. **For the fur trim** fill the cup of a sugar press with 10g (¼oz) of white sugarpaste softened with white vegetable fat and extrude the fur as before to cover the edge of the hat. Bring the point of the cone forward over the fur and roll a small ball of white sugarpaste to attach to the end of the hat (**B**).

2. **To make the nose** take off enough from the leftover paste to roll a cone shape and attach to the centre of the face. Turn the end of the nose up a little and mark the nostrils with the pokey tool no.5 (**B**).

3. **For the mouth** mark a smile with tool no. 11, leaving enough room for the moustache and open the mouth with the soft end of a paintbrush. Take off a small amount from 1g (⅛oz) of white modelling paste to roll a banana shape for the teeth (**B**) and set the rest aside. Insert into the mouth and secure at the top.

4. **For the eyes** make two small balls from the leftover white paste and add just above and on either side of the nose. Mix 1g (⅛oz) of white modelling paste together with dark brown paste food colour to make a dark brown shade. Take off enough to roll two smaller balls for the irises and press these onto the white balls. Roll two very thin banana shapes from the leftover flesh sugarpaste and attach over the eyes to close them a little. Add a further thin lace under each eye using the flesh sugarpaste (**B**).

5. **For the eyebrows** take off enough from the leftover white modelling paste to make two small banana shapes (**B**) and attach over the eyes.

TIP *Do not add the bottom lip until the beard is complete. You do not need to make ears as they will not be seen.*

The teddy bear

1. **To complete the teddy bear** you will need 33g (1¼oz) of teddy bear brown sugarpaste with CMC added. Take off 10g (¼oz) for the body and roll into a cone shape (**C**). Place the cone on Santa's knee. Push a piece of spaghetti down through the body and into the leg, leaving 1cm (⅜in) showing at the top. Apply some edible glue to Santa's hand and secure the bear to it.

2. **To make the legs** take off a further 8g (¼oz) and roll into a short sausage shape. Turn up the ends to form the feet and make a straight cut in the centre (**C**). Attach the legs to the body and arrange as you desire.

3. **For the arms** take off 6g (⅛oz) and roll into a small sausage shape. Make a diagonal cut in the centre and attach to the top of the cone (**C**).

TIP *As the bear is so small, you do not need to use spaghetti to attach the arms and legs.*

4. **To make the head** roll a ball using 7g (¼oz) of the teddy bear brown sugarpaste and slip it over the spaghetti at the top of the cone. Mix 1g (⅛oz) of white modelling paste with a very small amount of teddy bear brown sugarpaste to make a cream shade for the muzzle. Roll a small ball of the cream paste and attach to the centre of the head. Mark a line down the centre with tool no.4 (**C**) then mark a smile under the line using the smiley tool no.11. Open the mouth with the soft end of a paintbrush.

5. **To make the ears** roll two balls with the leftover flesh sugarpaste and attach to each side of the head. Secure by pressing tool no.1 into the centre of each ear (**C**).

Santa's sack

THE SACK

1. **To complete the sack** you will need 26g (1oz) of white modelling paste mixed together with 60g (2¼oz) of teddy bear brown sugarpaste. Knead the two colours together well and add a little CMC. Roll the mixed paste into a sausage shape then widen and lengthen the shape with a rolling pin to a measurement of 13 x 10cm (5¼ x 4in) (**D**).

2. Roll 20g (¾oz) of white modelling paste into a rectangular shape and place it in the centre of the piece you have rolled for the sack to help it keep its shape. Apply a line of edible glue around the outside edges and bring them together, leaving the top open. Seal the edges with your fingers and narrow the shape where the tie will be placed (**D**).

3. **To make the rope tie** you will need 7g (¼oz) of red sugarpaste, equally divided. Roll each piece into a lace and twist the two laces together to make a rope measuring 18cm (7in) in length (**D**). Cut off 1cm (⅜in) of the rope and set aside. Wrap the rope around the sack, securing with edible glue and crossing the end over at the front. Place the remaining 1cm (⅜in) over the crossover to form a knot.

4. **Add a small patch** measuring 1cm (⅜in) square to the front of the sack (**D**) using 1g (⅛oz) of cream sugarpaste. Make this by mixing together 1g (⅛oz) of white modelling paste with half the amount taken from 1g (⅛oz) of teddy bear brown sugarpaste. Set the sack aside onto a card, dusting with cornflour or icing (confectioners') sugar.

THE PRESENTS

1. **To make the red parcel** you will need 4g (⅛oz) of red sugarpaste with CMC added, shaped into a rectanglular shape measuring 1 x 2.5cm (⅜ x 1in). Roll out 2g (⅛oz) of white modelling paste and cut a thin strip to go over the top of the present. Make two small cone shapes and flatten them with your finger to make the bow. Attach to the white ribbon and add a small ball of white paste in the centre then mark the bow with tool no.4 (**E**).

2. **For the yellow parcel** you will need 8g (¼oz) of yellow sugarpaste with CMC added, shaped as in Step 1. Roll out and cut a 0.5 x 5cm (¼ x 2in) strip from 2g (⅛oz) of green sugarpaste and wrap it around the length of the present. Cut out a further strip for the bow measuring 0.6 x 4cm (¼ x 1¾in), apply some glue to the centre of the strip and fold the edges into the middle. Turn the shape over and pinch the sides under the bow to narrow in the centre. Turn the bow upright then mark two lines to form the middle of the bow with tool no.4 (**E**).

3. **For the green parcel** randomly mix together 2g (⅛oz) of green sugarpaste with 1g (⅛oz) of white modelling paste. Roll into a ball and use your fingers to shape into a cube. Add some spruce green paste food colour to 5g (⅛oz) of green sugarpaste to make a darker shade. Take off 1g (⅛oz) and set the remainder aside. Make three small cone shapes for the leaves and flatten with your finger, marking the centres with tool no.4. Attach the shapes to the centre of the cube. Take off enough from 1g (⅛oz) of red sugarpaste to roll three balls for the berries and attach (**E**).

4. **To make the amethyst present** roll 7g (¼oz) of amethyst paste with CMC added into a rectangular shape measuring 1.5 x 2.5cm (⅝ x 1in). To decorate, you will need to add some melon paste food colour to 2g (⅛oz) of white modelling paste. Take off 1g (⅛oz) and roll out a thin lace to wrap around the length of the parcel (**E**).

5. **To make the rose** roll the remaining mixed yellow paste into a thin sausage shape measuring 5cm (2in) in length. Widen the shape to 1cm (⅜in) with a rolling pin and thin out one side with your fingers. Roll the paste inwards to form the flower (**E**) and narrow between your fingers for the base. Trim off any excess and attach the rose to the ribbon.

6. **To make the candy wheel stick** roll out 2g (⅛oz) of red sugarpaste and cut to measure 4 x 1cm (2¾ x ⅜in). Run a line of edible glue down the centre and place a length of dry spaghetti over the top. Fold over the sugarpaste and trim with tool no.4. Roll on the work surface to narrow and take off 1cm (⅜in) of the sugarpaste, leaving the spaghetti showing at the top (**E**).

> **TIP** *It is easier to make the small rose with modelling paste, as it will roll out more finely than with sugarpaste.*

7. **To form the candy wheel**, randomly mix together the leftover red sugarpaste and 1g (⅛oz) of white modelling paste and roll into a 10cm (4in) long lace. Roll up the lace to form a wheel (**E**). Push the wheel over the spaghetti at the end of the stick and set aside.

8. **To fill the sack** arrange the presents on the top and secure with edible glue. Push the candy wheel down into the centre to secure. Place the sack between Santa's legs to complete.

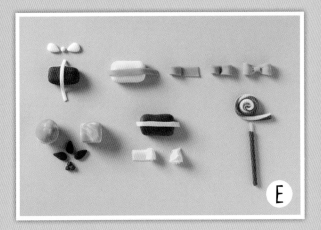

E

Using Your Toppers

When designing a cake you need to firstly consider the topper and decide which elements to bring into it to represent the occasion. It is always good to include at least three elements to give variation ideas for side decorations, for the board, or for decorating cupcakes and mini cakes. Here, I will use Pirate Pete cake as an example of how a theme can be developed and then give design inspiration for two further cake designs: Lucky Leprechaun and Scooting Lammy.

Pirate Pete

THE MAIN CAKE DESIGN

Pirate Pete is the main character. He needed additional nautical elements to make him more interesting, so I gave him a hat, pistol, sword, treasure chest and parrot. The small round cake represents his island. I love the bright yellow sugarpaste covering that gives the cake a warm and sunny feel, making a good background for the theme.

Next, I choose the shape and size of the board, which in this case is the same shape as the cake. I generally use quite a large board, as much as 10cm (4in) larger than the cake, as this gives you space to add other elements to the story should you wish to do so. In this instance, I have decorated the board to represent the sea, giving it an authentic marbled effect.

The side decoration of the galleon truly represents what the pirate theme is all about and I made a wave decoration to bring the sea to the edge of the cake. A few birds in the distance add to the feeling of being onboard the ship.

You can really get creative, have fun and run with a theme to create larger masterpieces. Here, this smaller cake could be placed on top of a larger cake, covered in the same yellow sugarpaste. The base could be trimmed all around with a border of waves, leaving the galleon as it is on the smaller cake.

CUPCAKES AND MINI CAKES

Cupcakes and mini cakes need to be kept very simple as they are usually made in batches. They are a cute addition to a large cake, could be made instead if time is short and they make lovely party favours to delight your guests. Here are a few that were inspired by the pirate theme:

These simple cupcakes are given the seafaring look with the addition of a small treasure chest, a pirate's hat and a sword. They can be made as simple or as detailed as you wish. You could also use a very simple version of the pirate to decorate your cupcakes.

Lucky Leprechaun

The gentle unicorn is the main focus of this topper, with the rider just as prominent. The magic of the topper is enhanced on this beautiful pink cake, decorated with sparkles and stars. Here are some further design ideas:

- **Decorate cupcakes** using the star decoration, with a larger star stood upright in the centre of the cupcake. The leprechaun's hat would also make a cute cupcake topper.

- **Decorate mini cakes** with the rope design around the base, embellishing with stars. The roses held by the leprechaun would also make a lovely decoration.

- **Create a larger cake** by placing the smaller cake on top of a larger one, trimming around the edges with the rope design, or placing a line of stars all the way around. A small bunch of roses could be placed on the side of the larger cake.

Scooting Lammy

This lovely green cake, edged with grass gives the impression that Lammy has stopped off on a ride to sit on top of a grassy hill and consult his map. The lamb is the principle character here and the scooter is also very prominent, but would be very time consuming to put on to smaller cakes. Here are a few design ideas that could stem from this lovely design:

- **Decorate cupcakes** using small, simple sheep or wheel cake toppers.

- **Create mini cakes** by shaping a simple version of the sheep from cake and decorating with grass.

- **Create a simple larger cake** by simply standing the scooter on top and edging all around with grass. The board could also be covered in cobblestones to look like a road.

Suppliers

UK

Alan Silverwood Ltd
Ledsam House, Ledsam Street,
Birmingham B16 8DN
+44 (0) 121 464 3671
sales@alan-silverwood.co.uk
www.alansilverwood.co.uk
Bakeware, multi-mini cake pans

Berisfords Ribbons
PO Box 2, Thomas Street,
Congleton, Cheshire CW12 1EF
+44 (0) 1260 274011
office@berisfords-ribbons.co.uk
www.berisfords-ribbons.co.uk
Ribbons – see website for stockists

The British Sugarcraft Guild
Wellington House, Messeter Place,
London SE9 5DP
+44 (0) 20 8859 6943
nationaloffice@bsguk.org
www.bsguk.org
Exhibitions, courses, members' benefits

The Cake Decorating Company
2B Triumph Road,
Nottingham NG7 2GA
+44 (0) 115 822 4521
info@thecakedecoratingcompany.co.uk
www.thecakedecoratingcompany.co.uk
For all cake-decorating supplies

Maisie Parrish
Sugarcraft Academy, Unit 21,
Chatterley Whitfield Enterprise Centre, Off Biddulph Road,
Stoke on Trent, Staffordshire ST6 8UW
+44 (0) 1782 876090
maisie.parrish@ntlworld.com
www.maisieparrish.com
*Novelty cake decorating, one-to-one
tuition, workshops and demos*

Pinch of Sugar
1256 Leek Road, Abbey Hulton,
Stoke on Trent ST2 8BP
+44 (0) 1782 570557
sales@pinchofsugar.co.uk
www.pinchofsugar.co.uk
*Bakeware, tools, boards and boxes,
sugarcraft supplies, ribbons, colours,
decorations and candles*

Rainbow Dust
Unit 3, Cuerden Green Mill,
Lostock Hall, Preston PR5 5LP
+44 (0) 1772 322335
info@rainbowdust.co.uk
www.rainbowdust.co.uk
*Dust food colours, pens and edible
cake decorations*

Renshaws
Crown Street, Liverpool L8 7RF
+44 (0) 870 870 6954
enquiries@renshaw-nbf.co.uk
www.renshaw-nbf.co.uk
*Caramels, Regalice sugarpastes,
marzipans and compounds*

Stitch Craft Create
Brunel House, Newton Abbot,
Devon TQ12 4PU
+ 44 (0) 844 880 5852
www.stitchcraftcreate.co.uk
For craft and cake-decorating supplies

Sugarflair Colours Ltd
Brunel Road, Manor Trading Estate,
Benfleet, Essex SS7 4PS
+44 (0) 1268 752891
www.sugarflair.com
*Specialist manufacturers of Sugarcraft
colour products*

USA

All In One Bake Shop
8566 Research Blvd,
Austin, TX 78758
+1 512 371 3401
info@allinonebakeshop.com
www.allinonebakeshop.com
Cake-making and decorating supplies

Caljava International Ltd
Northridge, CA 91324
+1 800 207 2750
sales@caljavaonline.com
www.caljavaonline.com
*Cake-decorating supplies
and classes*

European Cake Gallery
844 North Crowley Road,
Crowley, TX 76036
+1 817 297 2240
info@thesugarart.com
www.europeancakegallery.us
www.thesugarart.com
Cake and sugarcraft supplies

Global Sugar Art
7 Plattsburgh Plaza,
Plattsburgh, NY 12901
+1 800 420 6088
info@globalsugarart.com
www.globalsugarart.com
Everything sugarcraft

Wilton School of Cake Decorating and Confectionery Art
7511 Lemont Road, Darien, IL 60561
+1 630 985 6077
wiltonschool@wilton.com
www.wilton.com
Bakeware, supplies and tuition

CANADA

Golda's Kitchen Inc.
2885 Argentia Road, Unit 6,
Mississauga, Ontario L5N 8G6
+1 905 816 9995
golda@goldaskitchen.com
www.goldaskitchen.com
*Bakeware, cake-decorating and
sugarcraft supplies*

AUSTRALIA

Cakes Around Town Pty Ltd
2/12 Subury Street,
Darra, Queensland 4076
+61 (0) 731 608 728
info@cakesaroundtown.com.au
www.cakesaroundtown.com.au
Cake-making and decorating supplies

Iced Affair
53 Church Street,
Camperdown, NSW 2050
+61 (0) 295 193 679
icedaffair@iprimus.com.au
www.icedaffair.com.au
Cake-making and decorating supplies

Planet Cake
106 Beattie Street,
Balmain, NSW 2041
+61 (0) 298 103 843
info@planetcake.com.au
www.planetcake.com.au
Cake-making and decorating supplies

Acknowledgments

My grateful thanks go to Renshaws for so generously supplying me with their wonderful range of ready-made sugar and modelling paste. The beautiful new colours in their latest range have helped me make this book outstanding. The additional products supplied so generously by Rainbow Dust and Sugarflair food colours have enhanced the projects in every possible way.

The photography by Simon Whitmore brings to life the magical quality of my work, so beautifully staged together with the Designers, Victoria Marks and Jennifer Stanley. I would like to thank all the staff of F&W Media for the making of this book, especially James Brooks and Jeni Hennah (In-house Editorial) who have worked so closely with me, making this a very happy and positive experience and offering so much help and encouragement throughout. Special thanks go to Beth Dymond, Project Editor, who has added so many brilliant touches to the work in her own special way.

About the Author

Maisie Parrish is completely self-taught and her characters have a unique quality that is instantly recognizable and much copied. Over the last few years, she has been very busy travelling to many different countries, teaching and demonstrating her skills. She was honoured to be the prime demonstrator for the New Zealand Cake Guild, and became an honourary member of the Victoria Cake Guild in Australia.

She is a tutor at The Wilton School of Cake Decorating in Chicago, The International School of Culinary Education in New York, Caljava International School of Cake Decorating in California and Squires Kitchen International School of Sugarcraft in England, to mention but a few. She is also an accredited demonstrator for the British Sugarcraft Guild.

Her fans travel thousands of miles to visit her Sugarcraft Academy in Stoke on Trent, England, for a chance to be taught by the master. People find it difficult to believe she never actually bakes cakes for anyone, she considers herself to be a sugar artist who can visit as many as three countries in a month.

Maisie has enjoyed several television appearances, including *The Good Food Show* and QVC, is the author of eleven books and star of three DVDs. Maisie can also be seen on the Create and Craft channel, where she demonstrates items from her DVDs, books and kits. Further examples of her work can be seen on her website, **www.maisieparrish.com** where she welcomes you into **Maisie's World**.

Index

A DAVID & CHARLES BOOK
© F&W Media International, Ltd 2013

David & Charles is an imprint of F&W Media International, Ltd
Brunel House, Forde Close, Newton Abbot, TQ12 4PU, UK

F&W Media International, Ltd is a subsidiary of F+W Media, Inc
10151 Carver Road, Suite #200, Blue Ash, OH 45242, USA

Text and Designs © Maisie Parrish 2013
Layout and Photography © F&W Media International, Ltd 2013

First published in the UK and USA in 2013

Maisie Parrish has asserted her right to be identified as author
of this work in accordance with the Copyright, Designs and
Patents Act, 1988.

A catalogue record for this book is available from the British
Library.

ISBN-13: 978-1-4463-0272-9 paperback
ISBN-10: 1-4463-0272-5 paperback

Printed in China by RR Donnelley for
F&W Media International, Ltd
Brunel House, Forde Close, Newton Abbot, TQ12 4PU, UK

10 9 8 7 6 5 4 3 2 1

Junior Acquisitions Editor: James Brooks
Editor: Jeni Hennah
Project Editor: Beth Dymond
Senior Designer: Victoria Marks
Junior Designer: Jennifer Stanley
Photographers: Simon Whitmore
Senior Production Controller: Kelly Smith

F+W Media publishes high quality books on a wide range of
subjects. For more great book ideas visit:
www.stitchcraftcreate.co.uk